# WRITE
## THAT BOOK

*Guiding You from Inspiraton to Publication*

## Get It Clear
## Get It Down
## Get It Out

P9-CSW-039

Serena Williamson, PhD

First Edition

Book Coach Press

# Write That Book
*Guiding You from Inspiration to Publication*

## Get It Clear  Get It Down  Get It Out

Serena Williamson, PhD

Published by:
Book Coach Press
Ottawa, Ontario, Canada
www.BookCoachPress.com
info@BookCoachPress.com

All rights reserved including the right of reproduction in whole or in part in any form.

Copyright © 2004 by Serena Williamson

Printed in Canada

National Library of Canada Cataloguing in Publication

Williamson, Serena, 1948-
Write that book : guiding you from inspiration to publication : get it clear, get it down, get it out / Serena Williamson.

ISBN 0-9735207-1-X

1. Authorship.        2. Authorship--Marketing.        I. Title.

PN147.W54 2004        808'.02        C2004-902837-5

# Contents

# About the Author

D r. Serena Williamson, The Book Coach and creator of Book Coach Press, works with people who want to write a book, guiding them from inspiration to publication.

She helps people identify why they want to write a book and who their potential markets are. She helps them clarify their ideas so their book has a clear focus and title, and works with them to develop a writing plan and a clear timetable. Together with the author, she sharpens and edits until it is done.

Book Coach Press's artistic designers work with the authors to create a fabulous cover and original book design. The book is produced under the Book Coach Press label, while the authors retain the copyright and all reproduction rights. Next, Dr. Serena sharpens the authors' speaking skills and features them in their next Spring or Fall Book Launch.

Serena Williamson is also the author of *Surviving Organizational Insanity: Keeping Spirit Alive at Work*; *Two Voices/Circle of Love*; numerous poetry CDs; and the chapter "Write that Book!" in *Expert Women Who Speak...Speak Out!* vol. 3. Her speaking topics include: Communication Skills; Influencing Skills; Write that Book; and Add Professional Speaking to your Toolkit. Serena has a PhD in Adult Education from the University of Toronto and is a past President of the Ottawa chapter of CAPS, the Canadian Association of Professional Speakers.

Serena Williamson lives in Ottawa, Canada, and can be reached through www.BookCoachPress.com.

# Foreword by Dan Poynter

When I wrote and published the first edition of my book, *The Self-Publishing Manual* back in 1979, I had no idea that I would be receiving 15 to 20 books each week from people who had read it, been guided by the words, and gone on to write and publish their own books.

As an author of more than 100 books, consultant to the book industry and frequent speaker at writers' conferences around the globe, I never cease to be amazed at how many people want to write a book. Since it is my motto that "no one should die with a book still inside," I do everything I can to get that book out. My web site is jam packed with information on every aspect of book writing, production and promotion.

One of the services that I offer on that website is a reference list of Book Shepherds. Serena Williamson is one of those and I often send people who are struggling with book writing to her for guidance.

As Serena's authors will attest, she is a terrific guide who coaxes your ideas out of your head and onto paper. I am delighted that Serena has described her very valuable programme in this volume to help you with every aspect of your book-writing process.

With this book, you get to take Serena, The Book Coach home with you. I strongly encourage you to follow her thoughtful suggestions so that when you are in your eighties and looking back on your life, you can be confident that the words that you needed to express did, indeed get out.

Dan Poynter
www.parapublishing.com

# Acknowledgements

Thanks to Donald L. for fabulous graphic design and inspiration to write this book. Donald, you are my muse. I could not have done it without you.

Leslie Rubec, my Karate black belt friend and editor extraordinaire, thanks so much for your smiling face, kind heart and excellent work. You make polishing books a pleasure.

Dan Poynter, thanks for your encouragement, mentorship and modeling of what is possible. You are a guiding light for aspiring authors everywhere.

And most of all, thanks to my fabulous authors, the ones who have trusted me with their ideas, fears, concerns and hopes. Thanks for taking your journeys with me and for having the courage to write that book, stand up in the world and be who you are.

# A Word from the Author

This book was created to serve as a guide for you in writing your own book. It is designed to be inspirational, leading you to think about why you write, who your potential readers are and how they will be different after reading your book.

The book also has a practical element. It is one thing to be gifted with ideas, skill, talent and the internal urging to one day write a book; it is quite another thing to get around to doing it.

This book is designed to help you write your book *now*, while you have the passion and energy for the subject. *Write that Book* provides techniques to find your title and chapter outline, to create a template for your book, and to deal with days when the writing just will not come. It also tells you all about publishing and gives you enough information to ensure that you can get your book out there, whichever publishing format you choose.

Peppered with little anecdotes to inspire you, the book is filled with examples from people who have worked with me and are now out there, books in hand, telling the world their story.

I hope you enjoy this gift, and that it inspires, encourages and supports you to write, publish, and tell the world about your book. Please e-mail me at serena@bookcoachpress, tell me about your success, and send me a copy of your book.

Many blessings,
Serena Williamson
Ottawa, Canada

* Please note: The names of some of the people, whose stories are told in this book, have been changed to protect their privacy.

# Part One

## Get it Clear

# Chapter One

## Why Do You Write?

**So you want to write a book? Good for you! Why?**

Writing a book requires commitment and dedication, both in the writing and in the promoting that comes later if you actually want to sell some of your books. What powers your engine? What will get you through the writing and the even more gruelling promoting?

Viktor Frank[1] said, "He who has a *why* to live for can bear almost any *how*." What is your *Why*?

People who have a purpose, a vision, who have meaning, accomplish great things. Those without vision, plod along like zombies from day to day, accomplishing little more than their daily survival, or they unconsciously invent things to be passionate about, distracting themselves from their real mission in life by expending all sorts of energy on the little things.

## Jocelyn's Story

I had dinner the other night with Jocelyn. She has worked for a long time in a rather dysfunctional organization. Although she loves many aspects of her work, she gets extremely upset and frustrated by the petty politics and mismanagement that she sees around her. She is very committed to her work, and devotes countless hours of overtime that seem neither appreciated nor valued by either colleagues or superiors. Jocelyn is a young looking, vibrant woman in her fifties, and because she has been with this organization for thirty years, she will be eligible for a full pension in only two years.

Jocelyn is passionate about politics and human rights, but she has no time to work for causes because after all her stressful overtime, she has little energy for anything else.

After listening to Jocelyn go on about her frustrations with petty office politics, and because I have known her for many years, I said to her, "Jocelyn, you are a passionate women. You love a good fight and it seems to me that you are looking for fights everywhere to stimulate your passion." Don't get me wrong. I was not in any way diminishing her corporate stress. I know. I worked in a dysfunctional organization and was so stressed myself that I wrote a book about it in order to survive.

Jocelyn was suffering from misplaced passion. Human beings need a cause. We need a vision and a mission, and these may vary over the course of our lifetime. Some feel satisfied to have a family, buy or build a house, raise children. Others are driven by a singular cause throughout their lives, something beyond themselves. All of us reach times in our lives when certain aspects of our life vision changes. We reach a plateau. We have accomplished what we wanted to in life and are not quite sure where to go next. This is when we can get depressed or, like Jocelyn, discover that we have misplaced passion.

Over dinner, Jocelyn realized what was going on for her. She will stay at her job, and will continue to relish the parts she loves, but she will pay attention to when she feels herself getting riled up over small things, and ask herself what is *really* important to her, and place her fighting energy there.

## What About You?

Are you like Jocelyn, passion bursting out of you at the seams, when it really needs to be directed at your book? Chances are you don't have to worry about survival. You are not hunkering down at the bottom of Mazlow's hierarchy,[2] barely subsisting. Mazlow's original hierarchy described five levels of human need: *physiological*, which includes basic physical survival needs such as food, water, air and sleep; *safety*, which involves establishing stability and consistency in life; *psychological or social needs* for human interaction; *love*, which includes belongingness and the need to be needed; and *self-actualization*, achieving one's maximum potential and becoming all that one is capable of becoming and making a difference.

Chances are your physical, emotional and mental needs are met. You are relatively comfortable in life, and you are asking yourself about your contribution, the difference you can make in the world. Perhaps you want to enhance that difference by increasing your professional credibility with a book. Maybe you have a special personal story to tell, something that you believe people need to hear.

If you are here learning about writing a book, you are someone with vision. There is purpose to your wanting to write. So what is it?

Are you politically motivated like Jocelyn? Do you want to help people find abundance, spirituality, or happiness? Do you want to create better schools, help people raise their children, or reform the health system? Perhaps you want to make people laugh, or maybe you are looking for a safe outlet for your anger. Maybe you want to heal old or recent wounds in yourself and others. Why do you write? Maybe you just want to make the world a happier place.

## Writing for Self-Healing
## A PhD Dissertation

Mary writes to heal herself, and to heal people and the planet in the process. For example, when Mary wrote her PhD dissertation she chose that subject because she was in pain. She had had a spiritual experience, something that she believed was a calling from God and it changed her life. She did not know where to turn. Everyone she spoke with thought she was losing her mind, so she just kept it to herself, but profound changes had happened to her inside, and she could not go on with her life the way it was. She felt imprisoned by her former life and she had no one to talk to. No one! So she wrote in her journal, and then on her computer, and she read. Finally she had spoken with enough like-minded people that she began to find a community, but it took her a couple of years.

When she had to choose a dissertation topic, she could not do it solely for the degree; it needed to have a larger purpose. She wanted to help others who had had the same experience, so that they would not have to wander around in the wilderness for years wondering if they were crazy. She interviewed people to gather data for the dissertation, and in interviewing them, healing took place, both for them and for her. She researched and analyzed the data, and in the writing, she healed herself and influenced those who were working with her.

Although she never published the dissertation as a book, anyone who has taken it out of the university library and anyone who has heard her speak or read the books she has published since or even had a conversation with her over the years, has reaped the benefits of that research. Her children benefited, the people they came into contact with benefited and every person that she met and spoke with over the years benefited. Even if she had not finished the dissertation, people would have benefited. Would more have benefited had she published the book? Perhaps, but she was onto other things by then.

## Poetry

In an earlier career, I worked with cancer patients, teaching them to use visualization and imagery to help heal themselves. We looked at the stress that was going on in their lives six to eighteen months before their diagnosis. Most of the women were struggling with breast cancer, or a recurrence of their breast cancer in another part of their body such as their lungs or brain. If you asked them about their lives, they spoke about relationships where they felt they were giving without end, and not getting back. Get the analogy! The men had cancer of the stomach or esophagus. They could no longer swallow what was going on in their working lives. They had responsibility, but no authority to do what they knew needed to be done. It literally ate them up inside.

Coincidentally, or not, I had been struggling in a marriage that I felt was draining me. My clients were my teachers and, unwilling to become one of them, I left the marriage and saved my health. I never looked back, not even for a second. But that was not enough. I felt I had to help others too so I wrote about it; some conversations with God that was published as *Clipped Wings* and later, *Two Voices*.[3] I wanted to help others as I helped myself. But that wasn't the only book I wanted to write.

## A Corporate Book

The desire to write my second book was sparked by my last cancer client, David, a corporate vice-president whose stomach cancer killed him within only a few months. We met near the end of his life when he came to ask me to help him use his mind to heal his body. I wished I had met him earlier in his disease process. Imagery did some miracle work with the pain though; using his mind to relieve symptoms the morphine couldn't touch. Because of David, I vowed to get inside an organization, find out what makes people ill and write about it.

I got a corporate job, became mired in the insanity and promptly forgot my mission. Mercifully, a good friend pointed out to me that my spirit was gone and this woke me up. I remembered my reason for joining that organization in the first place, to go undercover and write that book. I succeeded and it surely did wake me up. I wrote *Surviving Organizational Insanity: Keeping Spirit Alive at Work*[4] for David, for me and for all of the other people I saw around me.

So my reasons for writing are very clear. I write to heal myself, to heal others, and by doing so, to heal the planet. What is the skyhook that pulls you forward? You are going to need it if you want to finish this project, not only finish it, but stand up and tell people about after you are done.

## Exercise:

Take a moment and think about why you write. How are you different after you have spent an hour or so writing? What do you hope to accomplish with your writing in general, not only for this book in particular, but for any book you might write?

Why I write:

_____

_____

_____

_____

_____

_____

_____

_____

_____

# Chapter Two

# What Are You Writing About?

## What is Your Hot Topic?

For some this is an easy question to answer, or they think it is easy. Robert came to me with a 64-page manuscript. He said he wanted to write a leadership book, gave me the manuscript and asked what he needed to do to turn it into a book. Because there are so many wonderful books on leadership already on the market, we had to help Bob find his unique angle. It took a few months of working together and playing with different scenarios for Bob to find his way, and then the book almost wrote itself.[5]

Heather was very clear about her subject. She is a financial planner who wished she could get her younger clients to sit down and have a cup of coffee and a chat with her older clients. Her book does just that. What she needed was someone to help her find the time to write and keep her project moving forward in her very busy life.[6]

Susan and Frances had no idea what they wanted to write about. They just knew they had to write a book. Ideas for four or five books swirled around in their heads and they did not know where to begin.

There seems to be one common problem for all people who want to write a book and have not done it yet. For one reason or another, they can't seem to get around to it. For some it is the book that has been hiding in the drawer for years. For others it is the idea that has been sitting on the back burner but they just can't find the time. For yet others it is the volume of information in their heads or filing cabinets and they do not know where to begin. For still others it is the inability to choose from the many projects that they are anxious to get started on.

## Start Where You Are Now

There is, indeed, only one place to start. That place is where you are right now. The books or ideas in drawers or on back burners do not get finished for one of two reasons. Sometimes we are done with them. There are two products to book writing: *the book* and *you*. If at a previous time in your life you were very interested in a project and you worked on it a great deal then left it in a drawer for five years, perhaps you are done with it.

One day at a business luncheon I found myself sitting beside a women who told me that she had a half-finished book project sitting in a drawer for years. I asked her what the subject was and she began to speak about women and make-up and makeovers. I could not help noticing that her voice, which was usually full of expression, was flat while she discussed the book. In addition, I had not associated her with that line of work so it took me by surprise.

I scrunched up my face and said, "Do you care about that anymore?" "Not really," she said, "but I like to finish things I start." Bad reason to write a book. I said to her very gently, "Perhaps you *are* finished with that book. Perhaps you have done what you needed to do with it and have moved on." She agreed and that unfinished project was put to bed, allowing her to focus on what was truly important to her.

So I ask you, if you want to write a book, what is extremely important to you right now? Stephen Levine wrote an excellent book entitled *A Year to Live*.[7] Dr. Levine noticed, after many years of working with the terminally ill, that peace often comes with the diagnosis, and so does purpose. The same situation happens in the movie *My Life As A House*, in which the character played by Kevin Kline finds true purpose only after he is diagnosed with cancer and realizes he may have only a few months to live.

So many of us live our lives as if the real living will start tomorrow, or next Tuesday, or next year, or after the kids are grown and gone, or after we find the perfect man, or after we get pregnant and have that child, or after we have a certain number of dollars saved in the bank, or after we own a home or after the mortgage is paid off or after we retire or after …. Often it takes a death in the family or a terminal illness or some other mental, emotional or spiritual thwack on the side of the head to get us to wake up. We waste years getting around to living, getting around to doing what we love and what we are good at.

Don't wait. I am not saying quit your job and go be a beach bum in California. I am saying that if you feel the urge to write a book about something and tell the world about it, start doing it now, on the side, even if it is only for thirty minutes a day. You will be flabbergasted at how much energy that half hour will give you. It may not start with writing. It may start with talking with people, doing some reading, research or just sitting still and thinking about it. It may even involve sitting still and not thinking.

## What Would You Say On TV?

Let me provide you with an imaginary thwack on the side of the head. Pretend your telephone just rang. Brrrring! You answer it and on the other end is Oprah Winfrey herself. She has just heard through the grapevine that you are writing a book. And since she thinks you are such an intelligent, fascinating person she wants to have you on her show exactly six months from today.

Oprah's advertising people are going to call you back in fifteen minutes and you have to give them, in a few short sentences, a description of what your book is about. If you do not answer the phone, she will fill the spot with someone else. Yikes!

So what is going on for you now? Butterflies? Nervous stomach? Did you just run to the bathroom and slam the door, or stumble into the kitchen for a glass of water? *Oh, no thank you Oprah, I am not ready yet. I don't really have anything important to say. I don't want to influence millions of people with my ideas and perhaps sell thousands of copies. I just want to sit here on my couch after a miserable day at the office, eat popcorn and watch The Price is Right.* Well guess what? The price is right! Thwack!

This is how you do it. First, breathe. Yes, breathe, deeply. Breathe in to the count of four, hold it in to the count of four, then breathe out to the count of four, all through your nose. Do this about eight times. Let your senses be filled with what sustains you.

We are not looking for a flippant answer here. You will be married to this subject for a while. You will be writing about it, rewriting, editing and rewriting. Then, not only will you have to speak about it on Oprah, but you will want to be generating and maintaining a buzz about your book for a long time afterward. What are you passionate about right now? What could you talk about for hours, with energy and commitment?

For Susan, it was her rage at her former husband who had left her with five young children and run off to another country with a younger woman. She had no idea how this would turn into a book that could help others, which was what she wanted to do. But she could help no one until this emotional abscess was cleared from her heart and mind. This was the fuel that fired her engine, and resulted in a great book.[8]

Always, *always*, start where you are right now, no matter how ridiculous or unprofitable it may seem. It will get you to where you need to go.

Now pick up your pen and answer this question.

## Exercise:

If you had five minutes on the Oprah Winfrey Show, five minutes only to give your message to millions of people, what would you say? What are you passionate about right now?

_____

_____

_____

_____

_____

_____

_____

_____

_____

_____

_____

_____

# Chapter Three

## Who Will Buy?

So you have just been on Oprah and people are calling in and running to the stores to buy your books. Who are these people? Are they parents? Dog owners? People seeking spiritual growth? Science fiction fans? Gardeners? People struggling financially? Baby boomers? People wanting career advice? Who are your readers? Think about them, what you want them to be getting from your book and how you hope that they will be changed afterward.

It will be very important while you are writing, to put yourself in your reader's shoes. Years ago, the very first person who asked for my advice on how to write a book was a colleague Bob Urichuck. After he completed his first draft in an amazingly short period of time, he brought it to me, as he did to others as well, asking us to read it and give him some feedback. It was a book on fulfilling your dreams, and it was full of exercises with each exercise built on the previous one.

Bob's book could not be read in one sitting. Well, it could, but that would not provide the reader with the most benefit. One had to work one's way through it for it to be effective. So I slowed down and pretended I was one of the readers. I did each of the exercises in turn to see whether they would work, and was able to advise Bob accordingly. Bob sharpened his already terrific exercises, made further edits over the years, and his book has now sold many copies in a variety of languages all over the world.[9]

## How Will Your Book Change People?

When I was doing my master's degree in Adult Education, we read a book entitled *Goal Analysis* by Robert Mager.[10] I still remember an interesting cartoon in his book. It showed people jumbled into two separate and distinct piles on the floor and he asked a question that went something like: if you could sort people into two piles, those who took your class and those who didn't, how would the two piles be different?

You see, Mager was making the point that teaching adults differs from teaching children in that adults are full of learning they have acquired throughout their lives. We must approach them differently than children, using and benefiting from their knowledge, and ensuring that they will acquire something from our classes, otherwise we are wasting both their precious time and ours.

So it is with your book. If you could sort people into two piles, those who read your book and those who didn't, how would the two piles be different? What do you want people to acquire from reading your book? Hope? Financial sense? Parenting skills? Fun and laughter? Inner peace? Leadership skills? The ability to cope with the loss of a loved one? The ability to let go and move on from a difficult situation? What knowledge or skills will your readers have acquired after reading your book. What are the take-aways? How will people be able to live their lives differently after having read your book?

In marketing terms, when we create brochures we take the time to list the features and benefits of our product or service. The features of your book tell what it is about. For example, this book features chapters on the various aspects of book writing. Now, instead of thinking about what you will do with your book, shift your focus from yourself to them, to your readers. How will they be different?

When famous actors appear on television talk shows to promote their new movies, they tell you all the features of the film. They tell you what it is about, which actors star in it, where it was filmed and perhaps give you some tidbits of information about themselves to get you intrigued. But they also try to create a feeling. The featured film clips, which are always included in the interview, are intended partly to show you who the stars are and maybe give you a glimpse of the special effects, but also to move you; to capture you, to make you experience something. If they capture you, you will go see the film.

So it is with your book. How do you intend to capture and keep your readers? What promises are you making to them? How do you intend that they be different after they have finished reading your book?

## Exercise:

After reading my book, my readers will be different in the following ways:

_____

_____

_____

_____

_____

# Chapter Four

## Find a Great Title

G reat titles spur us on. Now that you know what is most important to you, find a catchy way to say it. A great title consists of a few catchy words, perhaps a play on words, then a subtitle to explain what it means. For example, Joanne Thomas Yaccato's book, *Balancing Act*,[11] could be about anything — balancing work and home, balancing priorities at work, or some-one's history with the circus. It's the subtitle: A *Canadian Woman's Financial Success Guide* that tells us what it is about. Finding those catchy few words can be easier than you think, and are good to have at the beginning of your writing process. The subtitle usually comes later, after you have written most of the book.

There is a little exercise that I would like to tell you about. When I give a seminar or speech about writing a book, I always ask for questions from the audience. Sometimes I even ask for volunteers. While I was delivering a seminar at a conference for the Canadian Authors Association, one brave man stood up and told us he was having trouble finding just the right title for his book. I had him come up to the front of the room beside me and I stood slightly off to the side, facing him, my back to the audience, marker in hand, flipchart in front of me. I asked him to tell me about his book. As he spoke, I wrote down key words for the audience to see. When he repeated a word or phrase, I circled it. By the time he had been speaking for five minutes, there were about five circles around the same group of words. I asked the audience, what his title was. They all shouted out the circled words. He gasped, "How did you know?" It works every time.

Sit with a trusted friend, or even alone at your computer or with pen in hand. Tell your friend what your book is about and ask him or her to take notes. Or, if you are alone, take a clean page and write, in detail, a full page of what your book will be about. Then read it over. Circle the repeated words. During our coaching sessions, Susan kept saying things like, "I was so busy taking care of the kids, I forgot to *save some for me.*" I want to tell younger women to say to themselves, "*Save some for me.*" I didn't save some for me, mentally, emotionally, physically or financially." What was her title? You guessed it, *Save Some for Me.* Much later on, we came up with a snappy subtitle to explain what the book was about: *Inspiration for Single Mothers and the People Who Love Them.*

Heather, a certified financial planner was writing a book about women and finances. When discussing her book, she was always repeating the phrase: "*There's always something you can do.*" What else could she title her book? It was so obvious. That became her title, followed by a catchy subtitle that came later as the book took shape: *Women's Engaging Stories and Your Financial Future.*

Craig is passionate about career shift in mind-life, about people doing what they love and feel called to do rather than droning away unhappily in jobs they find miserable. He kept talking about the perfect workday, but he didn't like the word work. He preferred vocation. Moreover, he kept repeating the word perfect, and he loves acronyms – words where each letter stands for another word.

Finally, after listening to him for about two hours, I blurted out, why don't you just call the book *P is for Perfect: Your Perfect Vocational Day*, and have each chapter begin with one of the letters; e.g., "P" is for passion, "e" is for excellence or whatever. I thought he would jump off his chair in enthusiasm. The book was written within six weeks; this from someone who had been struggling for years with a PhD dissertation on the same topic.[12]

But there was no magic to this consultation, nor to the one before at the conference. Listen to yourself, really listen and your title will jump out at you.

## Exercise:

Talk to a friend, go to your computer or take a full page to complete this thought: My book is about:

_____

_____

_____

_____

_____

_____

_____

_____

_____

_____

_____

# Chapter Five

## Create Your Dream

### Find Your Model

Now that you know what your book is about, it is time for you to do a little dreaming and a little research. It starts in your own home.

Go to your home library and pull about a dozen of your favourite books off the shelf. Make sure they are books that you really love. Don't go into your head first and try to think about content. That is not the issue. We are going to the other side of your brain. Just go to the shelf, skim over the books and pull the ones that appeal to you and make a pile. Then review the pile for common elements. You are looking for colour, style, size, voice, anything that will give you a sense of what appeals to you in a book.

Now go to a large bookstore and head for the section that will house your book. Look through the shelves to find where your book will sit, and which books will be on either side of it. Now leaf through the other books on your subject to see which aspects appeal to you about the various books.

After you have done these two steps, you should have some vision of what your book might look like.

## Write Back Cover Material

The invaluable advice about creating your back cover now is gleaned from Dan Poynter's excellent book, *Writing Nonfiction: Turning Thoughts Into Books.*[13]

Dan suggests that we write the back cover material early in the process. This, next to your cover and title, is most important in helping buyers decide to purchase your book. You only have a few seconds to capture their attention, so make sure that you choose your words wisely. Writing the back cover now will also help you focus your readers on what the book will deliver and what it will do for them; that is, how they will benefit.

Back cover styles are relatively standard. Take a few of your favourite books off your personal library shelf and you will see the common elements. I will outline them for you below. With Dan Poynter's gracious permission, I have combined the concepts from his chapter six onto the following back cover template.

I have also used Dan's advice for the back cover of this book. Feel free to follow the pattern exactly for yours. Just replace the words with those that apply to your subject and your book. Between the template below and the back cover of this book, you should have enough to proceed.

**Category:**

(Where your book will sit in the bookstore. Go in person and check this out.)

# Headline

(A few captivating words – not the title)

**Description:**

(Two to four compelling sentences about your book)

**Benefits:**

(Four to six bulleted promises of what readers will gain by reading this book.)

You will learn (discover, be able to):

- X
- Y
- Z
- 1
- 2
- 3

**Testimonials:**

(A sentence or two from influential people who can stress different benefits of your book. Solicit from the best and offer them examples of what you might need.)

1.

2.

3.

**Your Bio:**

(Two or three sentences showing your absolute expertise in this area.)

**Sales Closer:**

(Scintillating sales copy asking the purchaser to buy.)

Bar Code
ISBN
Price

### Exercise:

Following the example above and the back cover of this book, design your back cover. Think about what you want your reviewers to say and begin to plan who you will approach, when and how.

# Part Two

## Get it Down

# Chapter Six

## Start Writing

### Maryanne's Computer

Now the rubber hits the road. There is really no other way to start writing than to start writing. It is amazing the excuses people will come up with to delay this process. It is like putting a damper on your soul.

Maryanne has been paying me monthly to coach her on writing her book. We see each other weekly for one hour and talk about the subject she is working on as I help her clarify how to tackle the project. Rolled into our contract is that I edit her work as she goes along. But she has given me nothing to edit. We have been working together for three months and not a word has come from her. Why not? She needs a new laptop.

Maryanne has a desktop computer but does not want to use it. She has pen and paper but does not want to have to copy over everything she writes. Perhaps she is just percolating ideas, and all will flow out in time. This often happens. But sometimes people make excuses. There is something stopping you from writing or you would be doing it and you would not need to be reading this book. Whatever that something is, get over it. There is no other way to write than to write. Period.

People worry that they are not good enough, that their writing is not good enough, that their idea is not original enough, that no one will read it, yet they are filled with this burning desire to write. Well then, write for yourself if you have to, but to spend your whole life saying you are going to do something one day and perhaps never get around to it can be awfully frustrating.

I advise people like Maryanne to write about where they are right now. If you cannot write, write that you cannot write, and keep writing about all the reasons that you cannot write and see where it goes. Before too long, this writing will lead you to your subject.

## Jennifer and Money

Jennifer has been struggling with money forever. It seemed to be her main concern, all the time. So she decided to write a book about it, to become an expert. She had no idea what she was going to write about, and she was certainly not an expert on the subject. If anything, she was a poster child for what not to do. Having no idea where her writing was going to lead her, and knowing none of the answers, she decided that if she was supposed to write about what was burning inside her, what was occupying her thoughts constantly, then she had to write about money, and begin to explore why it was such a problem for her.

So she began. She wrote about her pain, her struggle with money. She told her story, and the stories of others she knew. She called the book, *Healing Your Relationship with Money,* and as she wrote it, she healed both herself and that relationship, and helped others in the process as she discussed her writing with friends and colleagues.

Writing that book and promoting it turned Jennifer's financial fortunes around and made her wealthy. More importantly, through the writing, she healed her relationship with herself by discovering what was blocking her from allowing money into her life. She learned to love herself, and that made all the difference.

Start writing, with a pen, a pencil, a computer or a quill. It does not matter. And don't go to your notes. Don't open the drawer and start trying to sift through all your papers and previous bits of writing. That is yesterday. Start writing now even if you think that you have nothing to say or are not sure where to start. If you feel the burning desire to write and know that there is a book in you, start today!

## Anne's Handwriting

Anne's husband had just died. It was rather sudden. He had been feeling a little out of sorts, nothing much, just a backache that did not seem to be related to any injury. When he went to the doctor for tests, they found cancer. They did radiation and surgery, greatly diminishing his pain and giving the family some hope. But the cancer was relentless and he died within six weeks. After his death, Anne wanted to tell her story, in the hope of helping other families in similar situations and also in the hope of creating some hospital reform.

Anne is a very organized woman who has done a lot of writing over the course of her very busy, full-time career. Writing is part of her job and she usually finds herself quite at ease with it and able to produce high quality results that are greatly respected and valued in her field.

With this project, however, Anne was unsure where to start. Understandable. This book was going to be written from her heart and soul and she was used to writing from her head. She wanted to start with an outline. She had been keeping a journal throughout the course of her husband's illness and wanted to do a systematic approach, organizing her notes into a book, but she couldn't seem to focus.

When someone we love dies, we can go into emergency responder mode, making funeral arrangements, ensuring the rest of the family is alright, taking care of finances and doing all sorts of other things that need to be done. When the company is all gone and the house is empty, reality begins to hit. First there is numbness, then ....

Anne found herself unable to write with the ease that she had come to expect. Her mind was not in its usual mode. She could not create a table of contents and organize her notes since her head was all over the place. I told her to start where she was and to just write. This was unusual for her. She is accustomed to writing on her computer, but she told me that somehow, right now, she felt like writing by hand in a large spiral notebook. I told her to go for it, to just start.

Anne came back the following week with at least twenty pages written and twenty more the week after. After a couple of months, Anne had two scribblers full of her writing. Occasionally she would express concern that all of this would have to be retyped. At this point I would ask her if she felt it was time to make the switch to computer mode. No, she said, it was not yet time. She still had some writing to do by hand.

At a certain point, I believe it was when she went on her first vacation alone, that Anne surprised me by saying that it was time. She was taking her laptop with her on vacation and she was going to type up the book. When she returned, she e-mailed me sixty pages, and they were extremely well done. As she typed up her work, she took the opportunity to edit a bit, so it was really her second draft. The content not only informed and educated me, but it also moved me to tears.

From then on, Anne wrote directly on the computer. Her writing by hand had done the trick and she was on her way.

Don't wait for the perfect moment or the perfect words, or the perfect computer or the perfect sunshine because they may never come. That's not how books begin. Just start writing now and the words will find their proper place in your book a little later on.

## Exercise:

Get a notebook or your computer or go to the empty lines below and just start writing.

_____

_____

_____

_____

_____

_____

_____

_____

_____

_____

_____

_____

_____

# Chapter Seven

## Make the Commitment:
## Create the Time

### Not an Option

What a busy world we live in! Many people seem to be so frazzled that they do not even have the time to breathe. One of the chief complaints people make about book-writing is that although they would love to write, they cannot imagine how they could possibly fit it into their busy schedule.

I learned a valuable lesson about priorities when my eldest child was only four years old. We started Suzuki piano lessons. In Suzuki, one of the reasons they have such incredible success with very young children is that they instruct the parents to make practising piano or violin or cello a normal, non-optional part of each day, like brushing teeth. Would you tell me that you do not have time to brush your teeth, or do the dishes, or put gas in your car? We always find the time to do the things that we consider important. Isn't it amazing how we find the time to do chores, but often treat the things that we love to do as options? We also treat the things we need to do to nourish our bodies and souls as options. How often do people rush off to work and skip breakfast? They say they do not have the time, but actually feel righteous because they think they are watching their weight. Hmmm. How many people work right through lunch?

Once I was working on a project with a corporate executive who proudly told me that he kept his weight down by having just a banana at breakfast, coffee throughout the day and a large dinner at night. He was so proud of himself. He knew, as we all do now, that this is unhealthy, but he liked his pattern. But when we do not eat regularly, the digestive juices still flow within us and our breath gets foul. I wonder how this affected his sales quotas? I guess that is why we see all those advertisements for breath mints.

Eating nourishes our body. Writing nourishes our soul. Why on earth would we even consider making the bed or doing the dishes more important than writing?

If you are serious about writing a book, writing must become a regular part of your day. It can be on your schedule first thing in the morning before you get started on your other work, or during a mid-day break, or before bedtime. Believe me, as gas in your car makes it go, so will writing fuel you.

## Writing as Fuel

Before I started writing my book *Surviving Organizational Insanity*, I was not surviving organizational insanity very well. My job was killing me, if not physically certainly emotionally and spiritually, and I knew from my experience with cancer patients that if things did not change, illness was not far away.

I had put on twenty-five pounds since moving to Ottawa for this job, and I was exhausted all the time. I would drag myself home from work, with barely enough strength to cook dinner for the children let alone help them with their homework. I would fall into bed, almost comatose by nine p.m., and have a terrible time getting up in the morning.

After one particularly bad day at work, I could not fall asleep because, rather than being depressed, I felt angry, furious in fact. So I got up, went to my computer and started writing. "This job is killing me," I wrote. "How to kill your employees in six months or less" was the subtitle. Boy was I mad! I wrote about all the things that were happening to me and my colleagues in the organization, all the crappy things that were killing our spirit. At three o'clock in the morning I was still writing, and I was not even tired!

From then on, I wrote every evening, and my spirit came back. I soon developed a tentative chapter outline and a research plan. I interviewed people at work to find out what had killed their spirit and what they needed to nourish it, and the book evolved, as did I. Writing that book changed my life for the better, as writing will yours.

At the beginning writing may feel like a bit of a drag, and it will take discipline. But as you see the number of pages grow, you will begin to feel really good about it.

It takes a month to create a new habit so keep going. Write regularly, say two pages a day for a month, and you will see yourself change. You will become addicted to writing and love it. You will become energized, passionate and renewed with a sense of purpose. Your day will not be the same and neither will you. As a matter of fact, a word of caution is in order here.

Some people find that they become so addicted to writing and love it so much that the rest of their life begins to suffer. Please remember to save time for your family and other important people in your life. Their love will help nourish and support you through the process, so do not make them have to compete for your time. Save a special place in your life for them too.

## Save Editing for Later

It is critical that you do not edit your work as you go along. If you stop, judge and rewrite your work every five minutes, you will frustrate yourself and never get more than a page done.

There will be writing days and editing days. The editing days come later, and believe me, there will be plenty of them. There will be days when you go to write and nothing comes. Nothing. Those are editing days. Those will be days when you look over what you have done already, read it through as if you were one of your potential readers, and see what is missing, or what does not flow. There will be days when you think you have lost the thread and are not sure where to go next. You will know when you need to stop and reread because you will have no other choice.

It is important to listen to your inner voice. If you find that you cannot write one day, know that is a rereading and editing day. New ideas will come to you and the next day or the day after you will be writing with passion once more.

On writing days, just write and write and write, without judgement, without criticism and without editing.

Very soon into the writing process, ideas will start coming to you, ideas that have nothing to do with what you are writing, but belong in other chapters or sections. Good. That is normal. Your chapter outline is beginning to emerge.

## Exercises:

What time of the day or on which day of the week, and for how long will you write?

_____

_____

_____

_____

_____

_____

How many pages will you write each day?

_____

_____

_____

_____

_____

_____

# Chapter Eight

## Your Chapter Outline

### Capture Those Ideas

As soon as a chapter outline begins to come to you, write it down. Remember, it is not cast in stone. You are temporarily creating a structure within which to capture and organize your ideas. Nothing is permanent until you sign off on proofs from the printer. Until then, everything is moveable. But if you keep moving everything, you will never get the book written so you need to create a working table of contents as soon as possible, and stick by it.

The problem, and it is actually a blessing in disguise, is that once you have put your right brain into gear and you are writing regularly, you will find that you get ideas out of the blue, all the time. Ideas for new chapters will emerge, as will creative thoughts or groups of words that belong in various chapters. Great chapter titles and even the absolute perfect subtitle for the book will come to you at the oddest times. You could be driving on the highway, talking to a friend on the telephone, or taking a shower and you will get five ideas, all of which belong in different parts of your book. You now need to develop a process to capture these thoughts.

## The Post-it Technique

A good way to capture your thoughts for different sections of your book is to put each one on a separate post-it note. Then, as you post your various notes on a wall or board or even onto an open file folder, you will see certain ideas emerge as chapter headings and others as subheadings. You can move the little papers around and restructure at will. Post-it notes fit neatly into your pocket for travel and can even be placed on the counter beside the shower or on your bedside table. This is a great method in the early stages of writing a book.

## Separate Computer Files

Some people like to have separate computer files for each idea or each potential chapter. For some this works, but for others it is harder to keep track of what they are writing. At the beginning, when there is not much volume to the book, one computer file with page breaks at the end of each section works well. You can use Find in Word to retrieve your place in the document. However, as the chapters get longer and you want to spend time reworking each section, you may find that separate files will work best.

## Separate Paper File Folders

Since you may not have your computer everywhere you go, I often suggest that in the earlier stages of writing, as soon as you have a very general sense of what your chapter headings are, you create a separate file folder for each chapter, and get one of those small hanging file folders to sit on a corner of your desk.

Then as an idea comes to you, or a page of writing, which could happen at any time, even between phone calls, you can jot it down and throw it into the appropriate file.

## On the Road

Ideas will come to you everywhere – on the road, in the shower, during a meeting, over lunch. Trust me, at first you will think you will remember that idea because it is such a good one, but you will not. People have told me countless stories of coming up with the greatest ideas for titles, chapters, quotations and references and then struggling for months to remember them.

If you do not capture these fleeting creative ideas in the moment and cannot remember them later, you will want to kick yourself. Have a system. Pick whichever one works for you, and do not hesitate to change systems as time goes on and you outgrow each one, but you must have a system.

With my first book, I carried a little notepad with me in my pocket. Any time an idea came to me I jotted it down. You could even carry a packet of post-it notes. After a short time, as my thoughts generated new thoughts with sections and subsections, the small notebook began to frustrate me because it was not organized enough, but I still wanted something small. So I got a tiny ringed binder, like a little day-timer, only with blank paper. I made mini dividers and titled them for the separate sections. It was perfect.

I remember being a passenger in a car on the way to a ski hill when something great hit me. I whipped out my handy dandy little binder, opened it to the appropriate section and wrote to my heart's content. If it had been a standard full-sized binder, I would not have had it with me on that trip. Believe me, when you are writing a book, especially in the early stages, you must have something with you at all times to capture information.

If you like the digital format, a PDA (personal digital assistant) such as those made by Palm or Hewlett Packard and a variety of others can work well, and is certainly small enough to fit into your pocket. I am very digital and have not used a paper calendar or address book since 1988. However, I still prefer hand-jotted notes for the early stages of book idea writing. The advantage of a PDA is that you can download the file into your computer at home and do not have to recopy. The kind of writing I am talking about in this section is minimal. I am talking about idea capture — ideas for section titles, chapters, quotes, references, people to interview, etc.

## Digital or Tape Recorder

I have never been a person who likes to use audio recording. I am much more visual, but you may not be like me. Many people love audio recorders. They are great for catching your ideas while you are traveling, and are easier to use while you are driving. If you use an audio recorder, as with any other system, develop a method of transferring that information when you get home. Post-its can be popped onto the board, pages from the mini file folder can be popped into the appropriate file. PDA notes can be downloaded into the appropriate file on the computer.

If you use a digital recorder, how will you transfer the information that you have recorded into your files on you book? Make a plan and follow it.

## While Driving

I know people who try to take notes while at the wheel. Please do not. If you get a great idea while you are driving, have the person beside you write it down for you. If you are alone or with your dog, this is obviously not an option. If you do not plan to carry a digital recorder but do use a PDA, many PDAs have a short audio memo function. You can simply push a button and record what you need for later. If you are choosing a PDA, you might want to select one with this function.

If you have no companion to write your thoughts down, and have no digital recorder or PDA with audio, please try to pull over. Once you are stopped, you can jot your notes at will or phone yourself and leave yourself a message on your home voice mail.

If you are speeding along on the highway and stopping is life threatening, you will have to be creative. Have you ever heard one of those speakers who talk about magic memory games? They demonstrate to audiences that they can remember long series of numbers backwards, or the middle names of all the people in the room, or some other such nonsense. You can too. There are tricks to remembering things.

If you have a great idea and no other options to capture it, create a mental association. I used to help myself remember things by placing my watch or ring on the wrong hand. This worked in my twenties and thirties, but as I got older and my brain got more crowded (I like to think of it that way), I would forget why I switched my watch or ring. So don't use that method. This is how mental association works.

If you are trying to remember someone whose name is Carmen, for example, give yourself an exaggerated image of an opera singer onstage (as in the opera, Carmen). Look at that woman and see the opera singer. Guaranteed, every time you see her, you will get that image in your mind and remember her name.

That was easy. Now let's try remembering a more complex idea. Say you want to remember to talk about your trip to California in your book, and how that relates to a particular point you are trying to make. Give yourself an image of the singing group, The Mamas and Papas and start singing California Dreamin' all the way home. Or think of the Beach Boys and surfing or the song that goes Wish they all could be California Girls. Or if you are too young to remember either of these groups or songs, think of the ocean and surfing, or baking on the beach, and revel in those thoughts. Believe me, you will remember those fun things, and they will remind you of the idea you had.

Let's try something really oblique. Let's say you wanted to remember to look up a quote by a certain Polish writer. There a variety of ways you can give yourself a mental trigger to remember this. Think of red nail *polish*. Notice the many telephone *poles* on the street where you are driving. Think of a *Polish dancer* in traditional costume. Think of a *Polish friend* or political figure. Give yourself a mental association, even if you are driving or in the middle of an important meeting, and you will remember the idea for your book.

## Exercises:

What methods will you use to capture your ideas as they come to you while writing?

_____

_____

_____

_____

_____

_____

What methods will you use to capture the ideas that come to you at odd times when you are not near your computer?

_____

_____

_____

_____

_____

_____

_____

What methods will you use to capture your ideas while driving?

_____

_____

_____

_____

_____

_____

# Chapter Nine

## Start in the Middle, Maybe

So you have an outline, you have a regular writing time each day or a particular writing day each week, and you are getting ideas fast and furiously. Now what? Now you write. Some people worry that they have to start at the beginning and write right through. You don't have to do anything except write. Period.

Write however it works for you. If you prefer to start at the beginning and plough right through, so be it. I am creating this book about writing in order, from beginning to end, in one file. Why? Because it is an ordered process. I am imagining that you are one of my one-on-one, six-month book-coaching clients, and I am walking you through the stages. I need to imagine you writing your book, sitting here asking me questions and moving through the process. This project needs to be done in order as I imagine you completing your book.

My poetry was also written in order because it was written journal style, chronologically. It is an autobiography of sorts. Susan's book, *Save Some for Me* was also written in order because it tells a chronological story. However, when I wrote the book *Surviving Organizational Insanity: Keeping Alive at Work,* once I had an outline, I worked with each chapter separately as the mood took me. That book was written in the heat of passion fuelled by anger and frustration. I was struggling to survive in a toxic organization and writing was healing me. I worked out my solutions to complex problems in that book, and I wrote best when I was passionate about the subject at hand.

Do not worry about where to start or what you are writing first or second or last. Just write. Things you put into one chapter may later be moved to another. It does not matter. When we worry about perfection in the early stages, all we do is paralyze ourselves. The title is not cast in stone, neither is the chapter outline, and neither is what you write each day.  Start wherever you want to each day, and just keep going.

## Exercise:

Go and write!

# Chapter Ten

## That First Draft

### First Drafts are for Getting Down, Not Getting Good

Commit the above nine words to memory. They will save your writing life, as they did mine. Many years ago, when I wrote my first piece for publication, a chapter in a medical textbook, my co-author, more experienced in academic writing than I at the time, quoted those words to me when I was struggling to make sense of the volume of research that I had done for the chapter. He was so right!

Think of yourself as a potter. First you have to mix the clay and get it to just the right consistency. Then you have to throw it on the wheel and shape it, then you fire it in a kiln, then you glaze it, then you fire it again. You don't just wake up one morning and create a glazed pot all in one shot. So why do we expect that with our writing? The real fun with writing comes later on, when you get to sharpen it up, and make the words do exactly what you want them to do. Now I am not saying just throw the words onto the paper ... or maybe I am.

You have set yourself a daily objective. A best-selling author friend of mine writes three pages per day. When that is done, she goes on with the rest of her day. I have adopted this technique for myself. When I wake in the morning, after I do some breathing and meditation, I make a cup of herb tea and sit with my computer in my special spot. I take my laptop computer into the living room, which is brightly lit with the morning sun. I sit in my favourite spot on the couch, and I do not stop until …well that part varies.

Sometimes I write until three pages are done. Other times I write until I finish a certain section. Most often I write until I get hungry, which is usually about 10 a.m. The hardest part is to stop writing. When we start our day doing something we love, it is difficult to stop. What a difference from the so many years we spend putting off doing what we love until some time in the future. It works best for me to start my day writing. It balances me and gives me strength for the rest of the day. I suspect you may find this works for you too.

At different stages in our lives, we may choose to write at different times of the day. When my children were younger, the concept of trying to find some quiet time early in the morning was ridiculous. My writing time then was late at night, after they were all in bed.

When I was writing this book, I was working with a deadline. I had a book launch coming up for my other authors and three weeks before the books had to go to the printer I decided that I wanted this book to be a part of that launch. All of a sudden, daily morning writing at the pace of three or so pages a day was not enough. I cleared my schedule and wrote non-stop for about two weeks and made the deadline.

You may indeed find that the schedule you set for yourself is not working for you. Change it and keep writing. Whatever new time you pick, you must be religious about it, and you must also be rigorous about how much you actually write, and not stop until you have finished that first draft.

## Exercises:

How well is your regular writing time working for you? Are you meeting the goals you set for yourself?

_____

_____

_____

_____

_____

By what date will you have completed your first draft?

_____

_____

_____

_____

_____

_____

# Chapter Eleven

## When The Words Won't Come

### Editing Days

Some of my authors need to craft the words as they go along. That's all right. Everything is all right. I just do not want you to get bogged down in perfection and never get past the first ten pages. You see in movies sometimes, the frustrated author at the old typewriter, typing a few lines, ripping the paper out of the typewriter, crumpling it up into a ball, tossing it into the garbage can or onto the floor, and then starting over again, only to repeat the process until the room is littered with paper. Don't go there. That author was trying to write on an editing day.

Editing days are great. These are the days when you sit back with a cup of tea and reread what you have written so far. Be gentle with yourself. At this stage, you are working toward a first complete draft. Like the potter, you are mixing the clay and creating material to work with.

Editing days come up for a variety of reasons. The most common one is when we are staring at a blank page and nothing comes up. But there are other reasons for editing days.

Sometimes when you are writing, you will find that you have begun to repeat yourself, and that you are scrolling back in the document to see whether you already wrote what you are writing now. If you find that is happening, it is certainly time to stop and review. This happened to me one day with this book, but I was on a writing roll and did not want to stop. A paradox.

I was getting the clue that this should be an editing day, but was still going on. So I kept writing anyway, knowing in the back of my mind that I would have to take some time to read the document through later. Maybe the two sections would have to be combined. Perhaps one of them would be left out, or perhaps one would be a foretaste of the other.

Whichever happens, know that repetition is a key to tell you to take some time, perhaps later in the day when it is not your usual writing time and you have a cup of tea in hand, to reread what you have been writing and get a sense of where you are.  This is a good sign. It tells you that you are starting to amass some material.

You may notice that you have forgotten where to go next. This is another indication that it is time for an editing day. You absolutely do not want to force yourself to write. And you certainly do not want to write when you have lost your sense of direction.

I am not telling you to stifle your creativity.  Certainly we write from our hearts and souls and sometimes do not know where the writing is going. However there is a difference between creative writing and spinning our wheels. Trust your experience. Do not force yourself to write if you begin to sense that you are going around in circles. Stop. Go back to the beginning; either of the book or the section, whichever is giving you that uneasy feeling. Print it off, sit in a different chair and read.

## Stillness

People often do not realize the value of stillness, of stopping, of doing nothing. People will be working with me weekly on a book, and come session after session with nothing done. Sometimes it is procrastination, but often it is not.

Writing takes discipline and commitment and we certainly need to explore why we are not taking the time to write if that is what is happening. However, sometimes the times in between writing are very important.

Barry has been a member of my monthly writing group for some time as he works on his new-age fiction series. A very spiritual person, Barry is an expert on stillness. I remember a time when he went for about three months with nothing written, yet continued patiently to attend our monthly group meetings. He said he was percolating. He surely was.

People will work with me and not write for weeks or even months at a time. Then suddenly the book begins to write itself and in no time at all it is complete. Miraculous ... or not? The writing has been happening inside, quietly.

Stillness also happens on a smaller, more conscious scale. If you sit down to write and find that nothing comes, a powerful alternative is to stop, sit still, close your eyes and breathe deeply through your nose. Use the technique presented earlier in the book. Inhale deeply to the count of four hold it for the count of four and exhale slowly for the count of four. Do this eight times, rest, then do it eight times again.

## Get Some Exercise and Fresh Air

Sometimes our energy gets stuck because we need to move. Writing involves too much sitting on our bottom. Craig is a runner. If he does not have his daily run, forget about writing, or anything productive for that matter. When he is stuck, he throws on his running clothes and runs out the door. One half-hour later, he is writing at double the speed.

You do not have to be a runner to benefit from Craig's experience. Go out for a nice walk around the block or by the water if there is some nearby. If it is winter, you can even go for a short ski if it is feasible and close by. In summer, or if you live in a high-rise building with an indoor pool, go for a swim. Get moving!

Don't want to go outside? There is lots of exercise that you can do right at home to get your juices flowing. If you usually take yoga or tai chi or karate or kickboxing or anything, do some when you feel stuck. Just stop what you are doing, and do some right in your living room or bedroom or wherever you are. Just do it. Your body will produce endorphins, your energy will lift and you will return to your writing with energy, passion and purpose.

Don't do any of those things? Turn the radio on and dance! Don't dance? Well, fake it. Just jump up and down and shake your body around like a kid in kindergarten doing the Hokey Pokey – nobody is watching – it will feel great and get your writing going.

## Write in a Different Place

It may sound ridiculous, but if you sit in a different chair or go into a different room, your writing will change. If you have the luxury of a laptop, you can alternate where you write, even in a coffee shop sometimes.

One day while I was working on this book, I was so antsy that I could not sit still. I had to finish because I had set myself a rigorous deadline, but I really wanted to go out and be with people. I usually sit in the living room on the couch and write, with the sun shining on my face. I love it, and my writing is relaxed, introspective and meditative.

This day, I was in action mode. Usually in the mornings, first thing, I unplug my computer and take it into the living room. After I do some breathing exercises and sit still for a while, I open the computer and start writing.

This day, for some reason, I checked my e-mail first. I never do that because it sucks you in and an hour later, you are still sitting there, answering e-mail, with no writing done. But I needed company. E-mail does that for us. Oops, I had been caught! But why didn't I take my computer into the other room? It was a different kind of writing day, that's why!

I tried to write in the usual format, but it did not come. I was conscious that I was not unplugging and moving into the other room. Something was happening.

Well, when you get intuitions, folks, you can either fight them or go with them. I *strongly* suggest that you go with them. There can be lovely surprises in store for you. Actually, you will discover, as you may already have, that when you ignore your intuitions they come back to bite you.

I stayed at my desk, remained plugged into the internet, and even checked my e-mail now and then since I so longed for company. My mind even strayed once in a while to the cat that I was going to get myself for company.

As I noticed my mind continuing to wander, I brought it back, realizing that this was a day full of energy. I could expend that energy by going out and meeting people, or I could go for a walk, or I could do some of my Karate practice, or I could put on a record and dance around the house for a while.

So I went for a walk. I found myself almost running, so I did an errand, came straight home and went back to the computer, still at my desk, still plugged in, and I checked my e-mail.

Then I turned my energy toward writing and, wonder of wonders, my fingers flew faster than I can ever remember. I was antsy, not because I wanted to go out, but because I really needed to finish this book.

Book Coach Press's next launch was coming up and I wanted it to be ready. Like Jocelyn in the first chapter, my energy had been displaced.

I needed to write, but this day a different kind of writing needed to come out of me. Sitting in a different place, upright at my desk instead of on the couch, was bringing out another aspect of my writing that was not available to me while I sat in the living room.

This is the question of which came first, the chicken or the egg. Was writing at the desk making my writing different, or was I sitting at the desk because I knew, intuitively, that I had something different to say? It does not matter. All that matters is that you listen to your intuition.

When you find that the words are not coming, go to a different place. Take your pad and pen or laptop to a different room, or to the coffee shop. Yes, I know, if you do not have a laptop, you will have to recopy later, but it will be worth it. Your insides are crying out to you to do something different. So do it and see. A whole new perspective may appear and you will probably write things that you may not have written otherwise, and in very different ways.

## Write Something Different

When I sit at my desk, not only do I write at a different pace, I write from a totally different perspective. Words come out that I didn't even know were there. But this also happens spontaneously, when we are writing in our usual place.

If you are stuck and cannot think of what to write, go to a different place in your book. Sometimes we get stuck in a certain section, and we think we have to pick up the book exactly where we left off. This is not so. You may find this a particular issue if you happen to have been away from your book for a few days. You go to the place where you left off and you cannot quite get into it. Do not force yourself. Be disciplined and write, but do not force yourself to complete the sentence you left unfinished two days ago. If it is not coming, it is just not coming. Go to a different place in the book.

Review your notes, your post-its or your chapter outline, pick a section that most appeals to you and start writing. Again, do not worry about starting at the beginning, just start, anywhere in that section and write. It will all come together later.

## Troubled? Write About It

We must always write from where we are right now, from the heart and soul. That does not mean you cannot write from a historical perspective, it just means that your energy is guided by what powers you now.

If you cannot write because you are troubled by something, I can virtually guarantee that that very trouble will make a valuable contribution to your book. I have seen it with countless authors. It always, always does. You do not know how it will, but, trust me, it will.

Write your troubles. If it is about a relationship, write that. If it is about money, write that. If it is about the fact that you are lonely, write that. If you are frazzled with multiple demands and no time for you, write that.

Whatever you write about when you are troubled will morph into something that you can use. As you write, you will find that your emotions will begin to clear. They will either rise up and let you expel what you are holding in, or they will gently melt away. You will soon notice that your writing begins to change and you are drawing parallels with your book. You may actually use the troubled words you wrote or not. You may use them exactly as they are or you may edit the words so they fit into the book better. You may also choose to delete the troubled part and just include the part that is relevant to your book. Either way, you will have become unstuck!

## Change Clothes

How are you usually dressed when you are writing? Some people write first thing in the morning, right after meditating, and they are still in their jammies. Others go for a walk or run first, so they are in their casual outdoor clothes, others write before they go off to work so they are in business attire.

Other people write in the evening when they have some alone time. Others write after the chores are done, the pets are fed and the kids are in bed. You may not have thought about how you are dressed when you write.

Once when a client was writing some poetry and needed to bare her heart and soul, guess what she did. She took off her clothes, particularly her restrictive bra. I don't necessarily recommend doing this if you live with others, unless this is something they will understand. The Book Coach is not here to alter your moral standards. You will, however, notice that when you change your clothes, you write differently.

If you are stuck in your writing, assuming you are writing at home, get dressed. Chances are you are in your pyjamas or casual clothes. You may even be half undressed. Well get dressed. You have choices here, and the clothes you wear can vary with what you are writing and who your audience is. If you are writing a section of your book for business people, get dressed up as if you were going into their office. Not only will it put you in a better frame of mind to write a book for them, it will also, believe it or not, help you to see the world through their eyes. Go on, try it!

If you are still dressed up from work or from a meeting, and you are trying to write, you may find that your mind is still on the meeting, and that you are now thinking about things that you do not really need to be thinking about. It is amazing how we ruminate about things, long after our thinking about them can do any positive good. Get out of your work clothes, put on something relaxed and casual, and see how your worldview will change. Changing clothes can help you get unstuck and move on with your writing.

## The Food Conundrum

Sandra thought she had a food problem. She found that while she was writing, she kept going to the fridge every five minutes to get something to eat. That distracted her from her writing and interfered with her train of thought. Perhaps Sandra did have a food problem, but she was not overweight.

If you have a problem with food, and you know it, that is a different subject and you are probably reading a different book for that one. However, if you find that you are eating all the time while you are writing, you may benefit from Sandra's experience.

Sandra lived in a small one-bedroom apartment. She was very proud of herself that she had created a small alcove for her writing, a counter with her computer on it, a tall chair to sit on, and a file cabinet and small chest of drawers strategically nestled under the counter. Her telephone, fax machine and printer all rested nicely on the cabinet and chest of drawers.

It was a cute little office space, with everything readily accessible at her fingertips. One problem. Where was this little office located? You guessed it, in the kitchen. She was working in a small galley kitchen with her back to the fridge. She could turn around in her chair and without even getting up, could open the fridge door and snack. Yikes!

So she moved her office into the dining area. Still a problem until she solved it by closing the louvered doors that separated the two rooms.

Then Sandra moved, to a larger place with two bedrooms. She had the second bedroom that she could use as an office, but the dining room had a better view. Guess where she set up her computer. In the dining room, with her back to the kitchen, again, within arm's distance of the refrigerator. Mistake! Sandra lived in that apartment for a year. She got very little written and gained fifteen pounds.

This story does have a happy ending. In shopping for her new place (Sandra moves around a lot), this time she kept the fact that she needs a home office firmly in her mind. She chose a place with a second bedroom that she could use exclusively for work, a room that was far away from the refrigerator. In short order, she lost those fifteen pounds and wrote two books. But then she was faced with another problem.

## Remember to Eat

Sandra solved her proximity to the fridge problem and then encountered a different challenge. I know, some of you who are pounds challenged will wish you had this one, but don't be so envious. It can affect your writing and indeed your entire life.

Sandra had flipped to the opposite end of the spectrum. Sometimes we can get so carried away with our writing that we look up at the clock and notice that it is three o'clock in the afternoon and we still have not had anything to eat. We need the fuel to keep the brain going. If you are one of these people, you may have noticed that you are writing and you are hungry. You then ignore the hunger and keep on writing. Don't.

The problem with not eating when you are hungry is two-fold. First, because the brain does not function as well without food, your writing will suffer. You will reread at a later date what you wrote when you were hungry, and believe me, you will be able to see a difference.

A colleague liked to smoke Marijuana. He said it opened his mind and made him extremely creative. When he smoked he truly believed that the words coming out of his mouth and onto his page were sheer brilliance. Truth be told, the words and thoughts were drivel, more like the words of a schizophrenic, but no one could tell *him* that. We tried, but he lived in his own world. It was only over time, when he later read his words, that he realized that under the influence, he did not think or write well.

When you are hungry, you will not write well. Take the time to eat.

Another reason you should eat when you are hungry is that if you do not, you will get ravenous and then you will grab fast food items that are not good for either your waistline or your mind. Fresh, whole (not processed and pre-packaged) healthy foods make a difference. Good food equals great thoughts. Would you feed your racehorse pizza and beer at midnight? Then why would you do it to yourself? How many of us worry more about our dog or cat's diet than our own?

If you are stuck in your writing, check on your food intake. If there is a rubber band attaching you to the refrigerator, cut it. Make sure you eat regularly and well, and your writing will reflect it.

## Drink Water

Do you suffer from headaches, particularly when you have been writing for a while? Many people do and are certain the headaches are from stress or eyestrain. Perhaps, but probably not. The next time you have a headache, instead of taking two pills and a tall glass of water, have two tall glasses of water and hold off on the pills for about ten minutes. You will most likely find that your headache goes away and the pills are unnecessary.

Seventy-five percent of the time, when people think that they are hungry, they are actually thirsty. And being thirsty can also affect your mood and make you depressed. If you cannot write, get some water. Keep a pitcher of water, perhaps with a bit of lemon in it, near where you work. Please be careful to not put it in a place where it can spill onto your keyboard. My daughter Alison's glass of water tipped over and destroyed her laptop. That was one expensive glass of water!

If you cannot write, try getting something to drink, preferably water, and actually drink it. You may prefer to get a cup of coffee or tea, but remember that caffeine will dehydrate you. So if you do drink caffeinated beverages, you have to drink even more water to compensate. If you detest water, have herb tea or lemon water with a bit of stevia for sweetness. You can get stevia at the health food store and it has no calories. If you do not mind the calories, have some juice, and keep hydrated. You will find that you write better and for longer periods of time. And it can get you unstuck.

## Exercises:

What strategies will you use if you find yourself getting stuck?

_____

_____

_____

_____

_____

How can you improve your eating and drinking habits to keep you fuelled while you are writing?

_____

_____

_____

_____

_____

# Chapter Twelve

## Getting Practical

### Making it Real

You may be wondering why we have not covered this information earlier in the book. If you are a practical person and proactive reader, perhaps you are reading this chapter first. The reason we wait so long to get practical is that this section engages the left side of your brain, the logical, mathematical side. Previously, we have been stimulating the right side, the creative one. In my experience, often what keeps people from writing is the worry about getting it right—having the right computer, having the right office space, having the right idea, having the right amount of time, having the right amount of peace and quiet...etc., etc., etc. That is why, in the earlier chapters, all we are concerned with is stopping whatever you are doing that is getting in your way and just getting you writing.

Once you have some material behind you, some information down on paper, perhaps twenty or thirty pages, it is time to get serious. Now you know that this project might even become a real book. So let's make it look like one. The idea of setting your book up in this way and the guidelines for it are gleaned, again from Dan Poynter's *Writing Nonfiction*.

Most of you will be working in Microsoft Word, and since it is the most popular program, if you have the option, I highly suggest you use it. Since most people use Word, you will be able to get editing, feedback and comments on your work later if you and your colleagues have compatible programs. But you already know that.

Now let us look at page set-up. A good size for your book is 5.5 by 8.5 inches. If you take a standard piece of paper, cut it in half, and turn it on its end, that is the size we are referring to. They fit neatly into padded envelopes for mailing to customers and stack neatly in two piles in standard sized boxes for shipping. Plus you get a nice number of words on a page, and not too many to overwhelm readers.

Open your document in Word and click on *File\Page Setup\Margins*. Set your margins as follows: *Top 1.8; Bottom 2.3; Left: 2.5; Right 1.9* and *Header 1.3 inches*. Check the box marked *Mirror Margins*.

To create a professional-looking header with the book title and page number at the top of the page, click on *View\Header and Footer*. Type in the tentative title for your book, and press the space bar a few times. Next, click on the *insert page number* icon that is in the header and footer box. Underline both your header and your page number, and then set them in *Arial*, bold, 12-point type.

A nice typeface will give your book that professional look. Select *Bookman, BookAntiqua* or *New Century Schoolbook*. Last, click on *Format\Paragraph* and set your spacing to Single. You can also set your paragraph indent if you like by selecting *Indent: Special* and choosing what you wish. Now look and see what you have created. Your "baby" is beginning to look like a real book!

## The Other Parts of Your Book

Surely you have noticed that books have more parts to them than text. There are always pages before and after the main part of the book.

Creating these pages in advance will let you know what work you have ahead of you as you complete your book. Open a new file in Word and title it front and back matter. You will create pages for each of the following items. Please remember that the word page refers to only one side of the paper. A leaf includes both sides.

## Front Matter

### What Others Say About This Book

The first leaf of your book should be devoted to testimonials. You will be sending the third draft of your book to people of influence in your field and asking them to give you their reaction in a sentence or two. In my experience, they will probably ask what you want them to say so be prepared with a phrase or two that in your ideal world, you would like to hear from them. They will then read your book and see whether they agree. If they like it, they will move the words around a bit to suit their purposes and give you what you need.

Some authors leave this page out. It is amazing how many people want to know what others think of your book. Next to your intriguing front cover and sales pitch on the back cover, this is a very important part of your book to some potential readers. To capture these people, do not leave the testimonial page out. Gather your courage and send out review copies to twenty people, get a sentence or two from each one, and put their words and title on the first two pages of your book.

### Title Page

Next, write the title of your book, with your name under it. Leave out the word "by." It is obvious and unnecessary.

Below that, toward the bottom, type *First Edition*, since you will have many more, and below that type the publisher and location.

### Copyright Page

The back side of the title page is an important page in your book. Make absolutely sure that there are no typographical errors on this page. Here you place the copyright notice, publication history, ISBN, the National

Library of Canada or United States Library of Congress Cataloguing in Publication (CIP) information, the name and contact information of the publisher, and who to go for permission to reprint excerpts. Make sure the words Printed in Canada (or U.S.) are clearly stipulated to avoid potential international complications.

In Canada, you can get your ISBN and CIP from the National Library of Canada. In the United States, go to The Library of Congress. Their respective web sites will give you everything you need and they are easily found through your web browser. As soon as you know the title of your book, apply for the ISBN. You will need it to get your CIP, and getting a CIP can take a couple of weeks. Since you have to put that information in your book, it would be a shame to have the printing held up because you forgot to apply for your CIP in time.

Each time you revise your book, get a new ISBN and redo the cover and copyright pages to reflect that this is another edition. It will add credibility to both your book and you.

Do not underestimate the importance of this page. Those who know the book trade such as other authors, publishers, agents, literary critics and distributors will look at this page first. You will want to look professional.

### Dedication Page

Some people like to dedicate their book to a special person. I have even seen books dedicated to beloved pets. This is a right-hand page, and here is where you do it.

### Epigraph Page

This is for a special poem or saying written by a famous person or even yourself, something that has a special bearing on the subject matter and will touch your readers.

### Table of Contents

Tables of contents also usually start on a right-hand page and should not be too long or detailed. Use common sense. One author I know believes that chapters should be only two to three pages in length. In a 200-page book, that would mean that there would be 100 listings in the table of contents. Yikes! And that does not even include sub-headings for divisions within chapters. Create a table of contents that draws your readers into the book and helps them navigate to parts of the book that are important to them.

Tables of contents can be generated automatically in Word. You do this by setting heading styles for each of the heading sizes and styles you will use. Headings usually get progressively smaller throughout each chapter and will use a combination of italics and bold. These may be altered later when the book goes to the graphic design phase, but they are still important now to give you a sense of consistency and flow to your book. They will also help make your book feel real.

It is good to set your headings early in the process since you will use them throughout your work and setting them takes the guesswork out of which fonts to use for each heading and subheading.

Here is how you do it. First, pick the first largest heading in your book, other than the title. Let's say it is a section heading. Make sure it is in the size and typeface that you want, and select it with your cursor. Now go to the little box in your toolbar, to the left of the box that tells you what font style you are currently typing in. Click the down arrow beside that box and you will see some choices. Select *Heading 1* and click on it. A dialog box will pop up asking you if you want to modify the style. Click *OK*.

Now you can go through your document, select all your titles of the same value, pull down the heading menu and make them all *Heading 1*. Next repeat the process for the various levels of headings in your book.

Obviously your chapter headings will come next. Pick your size and make the first one *Heading 2*. Then go through the document and make all headings of that size *Heading 2*. And so on.

To generate an automatic table of contents in Word, go to the blank page that you have created where you want the table of contents to appear, click *Insert\Index* and *Tables\Table of Contents* and *OK*. Boom! You have a table of contents, and your book is looking more real every day.

*Important tip: If you ever do something that you do not like in your book, hit the edit/undo tab and it will all go away.*

## Foreword

It is a good idea to ask an expert in your field to write a few paragraphs about your book. It adds credibility and professionalism to show that someone important in your field endorsed your work. Since it is much easier to edit than to create, you can help this expert by writing the words for them. If they like your book, they will be happy to modify a few words and agree with the foreword almost exactly as you have written it.

Please be sure to spell the word *foreword* properly. It comes before the words of your text. It may feel like forward march to you, but it is spelled differently.

If the name is well-known, some authors choose to put foreword by... on the front cover to encourage sales. The foreword is also produced on a right-hand page.

## Preface

Also done on a right-hand page, the preface is optional as well. It is written by the author and tells why and how the book was written. If this information can be covered in the introduction or chapter one, save the paper and leave it out.

## Acknowledgements

Here is where you thank your friends, colleagues, coaches, editors, mentors, publishers, children, spouse, dog, cat, and whoever else helped make your book happen. People love to be acknowledged and appreciated so do not hold back on this section. They may be the only ones who read these words, but they will be grateful for your show of appreciation and will want all their friends and relatives to have copies.

As you are writing your book, add names to this page so you do not forget. Be gracious. They were your helpers, and also your supporters and salespeople.

## Introduction

Here is where you say what the book is about, why you wrote it and how you expect your audience to be different after they read it. It also mentions the layout — if it has an appendix, index, etc., to help navigate the reader. It is a brief overview of your book and it is usually written after you have finished your second draft so you know what you are introducing.

## Text

"Your first words should grab readers by the throat and not put them down until they have finished the book."

That is what I tell clients who have completed their first draft and are now looking at exactly how to phrase parts of the book and moving certain sections around to make it flow better.  Your text always starts on a right-hand page and of course, it is the main part of this literary sandwich. We will be dealing more with various drafts of the text in the next chapters.

# Back Matter

## Epilogue

You will add this section after the text if something has transpired since the book was written, something that needs to be included. If your book was a picture in time and you want to show the reader what happened later, you might put it in a epilogue.

### References, Footnotes or Endnotes, Yikes!

Being an author and a PhD, I am afraid that I am a bit of a stickler for references. If you put something in quotes, you must say who said it, and if possible, where or when. Nothing will destroy your credibility more than putting down a well-known inspirational quote and writing anonymous when it isn't. People will think that you are not well read. For an author, that is deadly.

For inspirational quotes, you can usually find the source on the web by typing the words, in quotation marks, into your browser.

Many of my authors write non-fiction books on various aspects of health, so they have numerous professional references. If you paraphrase the words of an expert, you can simply reference the book. If you quote that expert directly, you should state the page on which those words were written.

There are many writing style guides and each one will tell you how to format your references slightly differently. You can use a style guide or get your editor to look it over and write your references in proper format later. Either works. It is a sticky job.

You will make your job much easier if you keep track of your references while you are writing them and there are three easy ways to do this. The first is the APA (American Psychological Association) style. As you quote an author by the name of, for example, Jane Smith, right after the quote, type in brackets, the name of the author and the date the book was published. That's all. Like this: (Smith, J., 1990). If you are using a direct quote, write (Smith, J., 1990, p. 72). Do this throughout your book as you are writing, and then list all of the books, articles, websites and journals you used, in alphabetical order in the back of the book under *Bibliography or References.*

The other two ways to list references involve using *Endnotes* or *Footnotes* in Word. You will have to decide. Do you want your references to appear at the bottom of each page, at the end of each chapter, or at the end of the document?

To create endnotes or footnotes, from the main toolbar in Word, select *insert\footnote*, then select *endnote* or *footnote* and follow the prompts. Do this while you are writing, even if you do not know all of the publication information about the book. You will not take the time to find that information now while you are writing, you will go back to it later, but at least you will know exactly where to go back to without having to fish through the entire document.

### Appendix

The appendix is where you put additional information that might help the reader (for example, forms, questionnaires, samples of flyers, letters, and additional tables).

### Glossary

The glossary is another word for dictionary. If you are using words your readership might not know, include a glossary.

### Index

If you want your book indexed, you can do it yourself in Word (*insert\index and tables*) or hire a professional editor or indexer to do it for you.

### Order Blank

Do not forget to include one or two of these at the back of your book. People will photocopy these and pass them on.

## Make a Hard Copy, or Not, and BACK-UP

One of my authors found that it was very helpful for her to print out all of her book regularly and have a hard copy of her book with her at all times. That is your choice. At this stage of the writing, I believe that having it in your computer is enough, but you must do what is best for you.

One thing for sure, create a digitalized back-up copy of your work, every day if possible. That means, burn yourself a CD file of your book, date it. Each day burn another file and date it too. If your computer goes poof and you lose your data, yikes! If you have a hard copy your work will be available to you but you will have to retype it all. If you have no hard copy ... well, let's not go there!

## Exercises:

Set up your book as described in this chapter, so it looks and feels like a book, and has appropriate pages reserved for front and back matter.

Back up your work to date by burning a CD with the file dated today.

# Chapter Thirteen

## Discipline

At the beginning of our project together, I am very gentle with my clients. I encourage them to write whenever and wherever the mood takes them, to just write; in a scribbler, on a legal pad, on their laptop, or in the park. Just write. Now, however, you are in the thick of it all, and your book is a serious project. Now you treat it as you would a job, one that you love. It is not a hobby anymore. If you seriously want to finish, hopefully putting your work into book form has inspired and excited you. If you are panicking, breathe, sit down and relax. It is going to be great fun. Hang in there!

### Get Dressed or Undressed for Work

You may have written in your pyjamas before, but not now. This is business. If you are writing in the morning, get up, do whatever breathing, meditation or exercises you do to start the day, EAT a decent breakfast, get dressed and go into your "home office" to write.

If you are writing in the evening after work, get out of your office clothes and put on your relaxing writing clothes, and go into your office to work.

## Set Up Your Writing Place

If you have not yet set up a serious writing place, now is the time to do it. Some people take over the dining room table. I do not recommend this, even if you live alone. You still have a life and you still have to eat. It is no fun to live with a mess all over the place. Not only that, there is no door. You need privacy. In addition, dining rooms tend to be close to living or family rooms in which there are televisions, and are close to the refrigerator. Unless you have a dining room that is never used and is going to waste, or a corner of the dining room you can commandeer for yourself, find somewhere else. You will need to concentrate. If you have a spare room, use it. Take over a corner of a bedroom, or set up a little portable desk with your computer and cordon it off with an inexpensive self-standing screen. Wherever it is, create a book-writing place that is your own.

My two friends live in a small, downtown one-bedroom apartment. She is an artist and he is a writer. They do not have room to each have separate offices in their little home. If you were invited for dinner, you would not even realize that there are two quite adequate working spaces there.

In the left corner of the small combination living-dining room is a nice wooden cabinet. Open the doors of the cabinet and an entire workstation appears, complete with computer and file space.

On the right side of the living room, angled in front of the sliding glass doors leading to the balcony, is an elegant, inexpensive screen. Behind the screen is the artist's easel and all her materials. Creative, ingenious and practical. And you can do it too.

## Kids, Dogs, Telephone and that Cursed E-Mail

Get rid of the kids, the dog, the cat, the bird, the fish and anything or anyone else that might disturb you when you are trying to write. Of course I do not mean actually get rid of them, just minimize, if not eliminate your responsibility to take care of them while you are trying to write. Take breaks and take the dog for a walk or pet the cat and feed the fish, but when you are working on your book, you are at work. You are not home.

Unplug the telephone and turn the bing bing off on your e-mail. To do this click *Tools\options\e-mail options\advanced e-mail options\* and under the heading *when new mail arrives*, make sure there is no check in the box marked *play a sound*. Better yet, while you are writing, disconnect your e-mail, or at least turn Outlook off. You cannot write a book and read your e-mail at the same time.

## The Last Eighth

After I had been in the book coaching business for just over one year, I was talking with a prospective new client when he asked me what books my authors had published. I never stutter, but I did then. I may have been a great coach. But for what? If I was professing to be a *book writing coach*, where were the books? At that point, I had six clients with books seven-eighths done. Three had each worked with me for six months, were almost complete and had thanked me and said that they thought they could take it on their own from there. The other three were current clients. Believe me, that last one eighth of your first draft is the hardest part.

The beginning is fun and creative. The end can be drudgery. You want to be done by now and you are not. Not only that, you just cannot seem to get it good enough. Don't worry, absolutely everyone feels that way.

With these six authors I knew I had to do something drastic. This emergency situation birthed my company, Book Coach Press. It was the month of June. I found an editor and a graphic designer, called each of the authors and told them that I had booked a hall for October 3 and we were going to launch their books on that date. There they all were, standing on the edge of the diving board, with their toes curled over the edge, incredulous that I was actually going to make them jump. I set up appointments to see all of them and get them back on track.

Oh they all had great reasons. One was very busy at work and had no time (aren't we all?). Two had no money (now that's unique). One had a sick family member, etc. But they found time to write anyway, because I put the pressure on.

The home stretch in writing is not as much fun and can be scary. It requires focus, courage and discipline. The bloom is off the rose and you are beginning to fear your success. You have to grit your teeth and go for it. If you have not already set yourself a schedule, do it now, and put it up somewhere important. If you have done one, revisit it and make sure your deadlines are realistic; finish chapter one by such date, chapter two by the other, first draft completed by such date. Stick to your schedule as best you can. At this stage, there is no other way to get the book done.

## Four Drafts, and More Fun Than You Think

Yes, your book will require four drafts. That is why I say not to get so finicky about the first one. *Remember, first drafts are for getting down, not getting good.* You just want to get that information down on paper for you to work with. So your first draft is your best shot at your entire book, from beginning to end. Aim for a size of at least 144 pages including all front and back matter. Books under 100 pages are published but may not be taken as seriously as those that are just a bit longer. Do not worry if it is too short. Most likely in your second draft, you will find yourself adding material anyway.

After you have completed your first draft, I strongly suggest that you print your entire book out, get yourself a cup of tea or juice (I would not recommend alcohol because you need to be really clear-headed), and read your book through with the open mind of a potential reader. See if your book makes sense to you and includes all the parts you want in the correct order. Keep a pad of paper or your laptop beside you and make notes.  If you are really comfortable on the computer, it is possible to do this all on the screen, but you will have to make sure you have generated a table of contents as described earlier, otherwise you will waste a lot of time going back and forth in the document.

There will be many changes. That is good, very good. That is what second drafts are for. They give the book the proper structure and flow. Let yourself enjoy this part. Remind yourself that you are an artist. You have the rough form of your work, and now you are adding shape, colour and details.  This is the creative, fun part.

For your *second* draft, incorporate all the changes that you discovered in your read through. You may feel as if you are rewriting your entire book. Do not worry. You are not. Just because your book needs changes does not mean you are a bad writer. Remember the potter we discussed earlier? This is the fun part, making sure the book has all that you want in it and in all the right places. After you have made all these changes, it is time to reread your book again. For this read-through, you may not need to print it out. As a matter of fact, it is probably better that you do not.

In this next read-through, and *third* draft, you will be looking at the phrasing of sentences and correcting any grammar, spelling and syntax errors that you find. This is not a final edit because you will hire someone to do that. At this point you are not as concerned with content, you are looking at language. It is not so much what you have written, as *how*. Are you actually saying things in the way that you want to? Make these changes right on the computer as you are reading along.

After you have done your third draft is the time to e-mail or print and give copies of your book to half a dozen or more peers to see what they think. There are two purposes for this. One is to get actual recommendations for changes from people who may know better. The other purpose is to get testimonials to place at the beginning and on the back cover of your book, and perhaps someone of influence to do the foreword.

Don't be shy. Send your book to the most influential people you can think of, and send them an example of what you would like them to say. Most of them will happily agree.

Be sure to be clear in your instructions to your peers and experts. Do you want testimonials or critical feedback? These are two very different tasks with two very different levels of work involved. Some people who are asked for critical review, will just glance over the book and give you a pat on the back, and others will spend days and correct every comma. Be clear in your instructions, and know whom you are asking. If you want high-level critical input on the ideas in your book, do not ask your friend Sally the Speller. If you want an expert to review for accuracy, say so. If you want the expert to review for recommendation purposes, say so. People are usually delighted to help if we are clear with them. If you send a letter or e-mail to an influential person asking for a testimonial or foreword, the person might say that they are too busy or that they never review books. If you e-mail your third draft to the person and include a draft testimonial, you are more likely to get yes for an answer.

Please note, when you e-mail your third draft out for peer review, send it in PDF format. If you do not have one, you can purchase a PDF creator at your local business products store, and if you are a student, you can get a great discount.

In your *fourth draft*, you incorporate the changes that your peers have recommended and put their testimonials and foreword in your front matter and on your back cover.

# Part Three

## Get it Out

# Chapter Fourteen

## The Publishing Decision

### Royalty Publishing

There are three ways to go when producing your book. Royalty publishing, self-publishing or contract publishing. This chapter will outline what is involved in all three.

Royalty publishing is the kind of publishing that most people think of as the ideal. It may not be so in your case. In this kind of publishing, you submit a query letter, proposal and sample chapter or two to a large number of publishers who specialize in your type of book. Your hope is that one of them will like what you send and agree to foot the bill for producing your book, and even give you an advance against sales. You do not have to wait to finish your book to do this. If you choose this option, as soon as you have a sense of where your book is going, write your proposal. Whether you find a publisher yourself or work with a literary agent, you will need this document. Excellent resources on proposal writing are Susan Page's *The Shortest Distance Between You and a Published Book*[14] and Michael Larsen's *How to Write a Book Proposal.*[15]

## The Book Proposal

In a nutshell, there are eight parts to a book proposal. It is easy to do yourself, but difficult to do well. It is a good idea to get someone to help you with this because it is essentially a sales piece. It is what you or your literary agent will use to sell your book to potential publishers. It must really grab them or they will pass.

The *Overview* is the most important section of the proposal. It is your "sell" piece, and consists of two to four double-spaced pages, tops and should consist of six paragraphs:

- What's the pain out there? Why is there a need for your book?
- How will your book fill that need?
- How is your book original and different from other books out there?
- Why you? What, in a couple of sentences, qualifies you to write this book?
- How long will the book be and when will it be ready?
- Last, add a fabulous dynamic, closing paragraph, summing up the benefits of the book and its importance.

The *Audience for the Book* section tells who will be interested in reading your book and why they will buy it. You need only a page or two for this. Do a little research and quote numbers; for example, for a book on Being Single: there are so many thousands of single women in North America, and so many single men, this many thousands have been married and divorced a second time etc. You need to prove to the agent and publisher that your subject has an audience.

The *Author* section expands on the few sentences about you in the overview, and gives your credentials for writing the book. A page here is usually enough. If you do not have any or you think you need more, and we always think we do, get yourself some. That does not mean go back to school. Anita Flegg, one of my authors is an electrical engineer who has struggled with Hypoglycemia all her life. Finding no medical doctors who were knowledgeable enough to help her, she decided to become an expert herself, and write the definitive book on the subject. But who would buy it? Who would know who she is and why her information was sound? So Anita made a name for herself and established her credibility by joining Hypoglycemia internet chat groups, creating a web page, starting an e-newsletter and writing articles. You will need to do this and mention it in your author section. Tell potential literary agents and publishers how you are an expert and are in the process of becoming even more so, and how you are the definitive person to write this unique book.

In the *Marketing and Promotion* section of your proposal, again only a couple of pages, you tell all that you are going to do to sell your book: appear on radio and television, continue to write newspaper and magazine articles, and promote your book through your website and e-newsletter. You may even want to promise that you will do a massive Internet marketing campaign. In this section, you have to convince people all the wonderful things that you are going to do to get your book to sell.

In order to do the *Analysis of the Competition* section, you will go the bookstore, either in person or online, to the section that will have your book in it, and see what the competition is doing. Then you will describe, briefly, the five or six best-selling books in your field and say, in one or two paragraphs, why yours is even better and will sell as many or even more books than the others because of your unique angle.

The book's *Table of Contents* comes next, showing the prospective publisher that you are well organized. I learned this from doing my PhD dissertation and I teach it to my clients: as soon as they are clear where they are going, they must have an outline. An outline provides focus and keeps you driving forward. It also keeps you mindful of what you have left to do, and helps you stick to your deadlines. Having to do this for your proposal will get you clear. Find creative chapter titles if you can; they will make your potential publisher smile.

In the *Chapter Summaries*, take about a paragraph or two to outline each chapter. Even if you are not doing a proposal, this is a great planning tool. You do not have to write the chapters here, just say what each chapter will accomplish.

You will include one or two sample chapters with your proposal. They do not have to be in order, just the ones you like the best, or the first two you have completed, which are probably your favourite anyway.

Whether or not you end up finding a publisher, writing the proposal is a great exercise. It will focus you and make you even clearer on where you are going. The most important person that you need to sell the book to is yourself. When you really believe in both yourself and your project, you will be able to sell it to anyone. What kills books sales faster than anything else is the authors' losing confidence either in themselves or their book. Whichever publishing path you choose, the proposal is a good exercise. It will spur you on and serve as a reference tool throughout your book-writing project.

## Finding a Publisher

You can seek a publisher on your own or through a literary agent. Working with an agent gives you a better chance at an advance or sale with a larger publishing house. I have two colleagues who were able to get great agents and large advances in the United States. They were both Californians with good connections. I know others who wasted a year while the agent sent the proposal out to a variety of publishers with no success. American literary agents can be leery of Canadians. Oh, they like us as actors and speakers, but they sometimes question whether, as writers, we have sufficient knowledge of the vast United States market. If you choose to play on the American turf, you must be prepared to convince them that you can.

In Canada, advances for first time authors are extremely rare and quite minimal. You can check out publishers and agents at www.writersmarket.com, to which you can subscribe very reasonably. For free, you can use the printed version in the library. This is a fabulous, comprehensive resource and it is updated regularly.

A good way to find a publisher or an agent is to go to the bookstore, to the shelf where your book would sit and look at who publishes books in your genre. Look also at the acknowledgements. Often the author thanks his or her agent. Make a list of potential publishers and agents. You can then look up their co-ordinates in Writers Market and pitch them.

## Where's the Dough?

The publisher pays all the upfront costs of producing the book. The reason this is called Royalty publishing is that you get royalties. Once the books begin to sell, you get ten percent of the cover price, either wholesale or retail, depending on your contract. The publisher will put your book in a catalogue and into one or two of the main online bookstores. Their sales people or their distributor will promote your book, along with all the others in their catalogue for that season, to bookstores. The buyer will either take a couple of copies or pass. Period. The rest of the marketing is up to you. Your publisher will give you an agreed-upon number of free copies, say ten or twenty, and you have to buy the rest at an agreed upon discount price. Six months later, you are yesterday's news, relegated to the back of the catalogue or out of it altogether. All other marketing is up to you.

All bookstore sales go through the publisher and their distributor and they retain the rights to reproduce your book. If you choose this method of publishing, please have someone knowledgeable look over your contract before you sign. You want to retain the copyright to your material and the right to reproduce it in other forms. There are many horror stories and you do not want to be one of them.

Last, but certainly not least, royalty publishing takes time. Allow at least a year if not more before you see your book in print. It will usually take your agent at least six months to get a bite, if at all. If you or your agent should magically sell your book idea quickly, fabulous! Your publisher will give you deadlines to get your book written. If, however you are hot about your topic and want to get your book out to market soon, you may want to consider one of the two options below, self or contract publishing.

## Self-Publishing

Self-publishing is far easier than you might expect, and less expensive. And you retain all the rights and control of the product. You can reproduce it in any format you like — CDs, e-books, on-line learning ... anything, and you have control of how much profit you make.

You will have to put together a team consisting of editor, graphic designer and printer, which is not so hard and will be discussed further in the next section. You have to pay the upfront costs, but you will probably make more money, and sooner.

Costs for production will vary depending on the quantity you produce. There is print on demand publishing, which can produce, say 50 or 100 copies at a time. This requires little initial financial outlay, but costs you much more per book. With quantities of around 2,000, you can reduce your costs to as low as $3.00 CDN each for books which will sell for $20.00. That is $26,000.00 profit. And reprinting costs less. Think about it.

You can choose to sell your books at the back of the room when you speak or on your website and all the profit is yours. You can also be like the big publishers and convince bookstores to carry your book. They will want a 40 percent discount. You can also hire a distributor as the big publishers do and they will put you in their catalogue and promote you to bookstores. They take 25 percent. Are you doing the math?

What this all boils down to is that books do not sell more if they happen to be sitting on a bookstore shelf rather than on your website. What sells books is you making a noise about them, everywhere and often. We will discuss this a little further in the chapter on marketing.

If you are a first-time author, I highly recommend publishing your book yourself rather than searching for a publisher or an agent. You get it done now, while you are still passionate about the topic. It is you who has to do the marketing anyway, and you can hire whatever you need in terms of distribution, etc. This way, you have control of the product. If you are giving a big presentation and need fifty books, you just grab a box from your basement, garage or closet and off you go. If you make a really big noise about your book and sell lots of copies, the publishers will find you, and then you will be in the driver's seat about royalty advances.

Maybe even two publishers will want your book and you can get a price war going. Your loving the subject, having confidence in yourself and making a commotion about it because you really believe in your book, is what is going to sell it, not who published it and where the boxes live.

## Vanity or Subsidy Publishing

This form of publishing is self-publishing with a middleperson. Originally, this form of publishing was called vanity press, which had a bad name because some companies would slap a cover on and publish just about anything. The quality was quite poor. They would also promise all sorts of marketing advantages, then often not live up to their promises. If a deal sounds too good to be true, it probably is. The prices you pay are often more than you would pay for the same services if you went directly to them. You will, with a vanity press, need to ensure that copyright and all reproduction rights are in your name. Look at how much money they are going to make on this deal, and let that be your guide.

## Contract Publishing or Book Shepherds

With this form of publishing, you have the benefit of a production coach and manager, someone who has all the connections with graphic design, editing and printing, and can help you get your book out with little or no hassle. They will make no promises to market or sell your book, just to help you get it done. The copyright and all reproduction rights will be in your name. A reputable contract publishing firm will get less expensive prices from graphic designers, editors and printers because of the volume they produce and they will pass these savings on to you.

As an extension of our Book Coaching services, I launched Book Coach Press as a contract publishing company. I did this for two reasons. First, I needed to push my authors to press because they were struck at seven-eighths done. Second, the prices my authors were getting for self-publishing off the street were astronomical. I know what the actual costs were and I knew that by working in bulk, I could do better for them. Opening Book Coach Press was a work of the heart and soul and a gift to my authors.

J.P. and R.W. considered using our services to coach them through their book writing, editing and production, but decided that they could go it alone.  When it came time to produce their books, they went to our website to find out who we use for editing and graphic design and went straight to them. They paid off the street prices, and it cost them much more to produce their books than if they had gone through us. Do your numbers. If a contract publisher saves you hassle and money, and does not make a wagonload of promises, they might be the ones for you.

## Exercises:

How do you want to produce your book?

_____

_____

_____

_____

_____

Who do you want to be in charge?

_____

_____

_____

_____

_____

# Chapter Fifteen

## Self-Publishing Nuts, Bolts and Possibilities

### The Printed Book

So you have chosen to publish your book yourself. Good for you! Let me be a shepherd for you and provide a guide that will help you through some of the steps. Have fun and enjoy the process!

### Use a Professional Editor

Never, never, *never* send your book to print without having a professional editor look at it. You will not believe how many errors they will find on each page. You will be astounded!

Ask around. Your colleagues may know professional editors. There are also Editors Associations in both Canada and the United States. They have local chapters in most cities and the locations are listed on their websites. Your Internet browser will direct you to the current website for the Editors' Association of Canada or the corresponding one in the United States.

Again, be clear about what you want from your editor. *Substantive* editing involves reorganizing sections and rewriting text. *Copyediting* involves checking for spelling, grammar and syntax. *Proof-reading* involves just that; reading over the proofs from the printer to ensure that there are no last minute errors going to print. If you do not want your editor to recommend major changes, say so, or you may find your book restructured in ways that you may not have wanted.

If you are concerned about your ability to write, it is a good idea to be working with a coach from the beginning, so he or she can edit your work as you go along. You may want to use the services of a substantive editor to help you organize your work. If however, you are relatively comfortable with your writing, a copyeditor will be enough. You absolutely must be willing to pay for them to go over your book at least three times.

The editor will get your book for the first time after you and your peers have taken it as far as you can, that is, after your fourth draft. He or she will find tons of little mistakes. Either you or the editor will enter these changes into your document. Then you are ready to go to graphic design.

## Graphic Design

The saying goes that you can't judge a book by its cover, but unfortunately most people do. A well-designed cover will be artistic, creative and give hints at what the book is about. A great cover design will do two things. It will attract people to your book and it will indicate the degree of professionalism with which your book has been written. The investment is well worth the money. Shop around. Ask to see other work that the designer has done. A serious designer will take the time to read the book through and see what it is about to get a feel for it. He or she will interview you to get a sense of what is special to you about the book, and if there are images or colours that have special meaning for you.

Since Allyson had worked with me on the creation of her book, when she was ready, we went to see the graphic designer together. We had given him the book to read in advance so he had a good sense of the content. While we were chatting, I said to Allyson, "Tell Don about the Monarch."

Allyson went very quiet and tears came to her eyes. "My God," she finally said when she found her voice, "Could we really put a Monarch on the cover of the book." Of course we could — we could do anything. The Monarch butterfly had been an extremely important image to Allyson and had given her much comfort in her life. Of course the designer would find a way to incorporate the Monarch onto her cover.

I then asked Allyson to tell the designer about the colour red/orange. Same reaction. Her book, *The Path to Cure*[16] has a lovely cover using the red/orange colour, the Monarch butterfly, and her son, Jordan, whose illness led her to discover new healing paths and changed her life. Do not skimp on the cover. Use a professional graphic designer and remember that you get what you pay for.

The graphic designer will also format the inside of your book. He or she will ensure that the type is easy to read and spaced nicely on the page. The graphic designer will select fonts to match the style of your writing and, in general, give your book a professional look and feel. If you really like desktop publishing, you might be able to do this yourself, but if you are a writer, why don't you stick to your own craft and let a professional do it. When authors skimp on graphic design, it shows, and you cannot take the book back after it is out there in print.

After the graphic designer has formatted the text of your book, it goes to the editor for the second round, then the graphic designer, not you, inputs the changes into the designed formatted text. This must be careful work. The insertion of even a period can throw the whole page off. A professional designer will know how to do this properly. Then off you go to print.

## Printing

Go to a few different printers and get prices. By this time you will know exactly how big your book will be. You will have your sample in hand, the kind of cover you want, the thickness of the pages, etc. You and your graphic designer will have made all those decisions already based on the book shopping you did earlier when you chose the ideal look, shape and feel of your book. Your graphic designer will also be able to talk to you about paper quality and page thickness so that you can go to the printer with specifications in hand. He or she may also have experience with different printing companies and be able to make recommendations.

Ask around. See who has worked with which companies and who has a reputation for good quality printing and go with them.

The more you produce, the cheaper the cost per book, so think seriously about how many of your books you believe you can sell. Maybe it is a good idea to print only 500, pay more for each copy, and see how you do  promoting them. If your book takes off and you love the promotion part, you can print a few thousand next time around, and write on the copyright page Second Printing or Second Edition. This also gives you the opportunity to make a few changes — which you surely will because we authors always find things to correct, change or add the minute the book is off the press.

On the other hand, you are spending good money for graphic design and editing, so you want to get the biggest bang for your buck by printing as many as you can at one time. When you print many books, they cost as little as four colour brochures do, and make much better marketing tools.

Also, take into consideration, that when you go to reprint, your design and editing costs will already have been paid for.

## E-Books

You can be an author without even going to print. Create your book in Word, get a great cover done, convert it to PDF format with a PDF creator, then post it on your website. Bing, you're an author. You can also sell your printed book in digital format on your website.

## Audio Books

I wanted to publish my poetry in audio format so people could hear me reading it, and also because I wanted something published right away and did not want to go through the expense of the printed book.

For an investment of under $100.00, I created four audio CDs, and I did it all on my little laptop computer. You can do it too. I went to my local business store — you know, the big supermarket kind, and asked a knowledgeable young salesperson what I needed to record and edit audio. He recommended Sound Forge XP, which I bought for less than $20.00, and a good headset microphone, which cost $39.00.

I sat at my little laptop, at a table overlooking the ocean while on vacation in Florida, and recorded my poetry with real ocean sounds in the background. I duplicated the CDs myself at home, on demand, and made my own labels. When orders got bigger, I asked around and found someone to duplicate and label them for me. You can do the same.

You do not even have to create actual CDs to make money from your ideas. You can have your audio files directly downloadable, for a fee, from your website. Cha-ching, money in the bank! Your web designer can tell you how to do this.

I spoke last night at a meeting of the Canadian Authors Association. One of the authors, a poet, was asking me how to format her document on the computer because her friend, a "publisher" wanted it camera ready. I asked her if her friend was a publisher or just a printer. A publisher would have graphic designers to format poetry and would not expect an author to do it herself.

You may like to fiddle with technical things, I know I do, but you have to decide what is the best use of your time. You can spend months learning how to create a website or downloadable files on the computer, when an expert could do it in much less time, in a far more professional way, while you get on with the business of writing. I advised this woman, who confessed to being almost computer illiterate, to spend her time writing more poems and leave the designing to the experts. So it is with downloadable audio and e-products. Get an expert to set it up for you, if possible, in a way that you can upload future items yourself. If not, better to have it done professionally for a few extra dollars than to look unprofessional.

## CD Sets

Compact disc sets are a great way to get your information out and make a few dollars. A potential client approached me recently with a manual that was chock full of information. She wanted to turn it into a book. When I looked at it, I realized that it was a potential CD or DVD set. Since she is an expert in interactive web learning, this step was a natural. CD or interactive DVD sets can sell for prices like $199.00. We did some math. If she did a massive internet marketing campaign with the aim of selling, say 10,000 copies. That is almost two million dollars. We both stared open-mouthed at the calculator.

## Exercise:

Dream. What other products could you produce with your material in addition to your book?

_____

_____

_____

_____

_____

How much will you do yourself, and what will you get help with?

_____

_____

_____

_____

_____

_____

_____

# Chapter Sixteen

## To Market, To Market

### Where's the Dough?

Some people say that there is no money in book production. Get out there and do business, they say, don't sit at home at the computer writing. They are partially right. There is no money in book writing if your only aim is to write the book.

After you have written your book, you have completed one phase. You have poured your heart and soul and brain onto paper, CD or your website, or all three. Somehow a funny thing happens after people have produced their work. They think that it will sell itself. Sorry, it will not. Even if you have great distribution and there are copies of your book in every bookstore across the continent, how are the books on the bookstores shelves different from the ones in boxes in the warehouse or your garage? There is really no difference at all except location. If you do not make a noise about your books, they will stay where they are, wherever that is. Bookstores return books that are not selling and expect a refund.

No matter who publishes your book, you are now in a different phase. If you are like most writers, in your mind, you are now finished with this project and want to get on with your next book. Great, go for it, but something has to be done, by you, to get your current book out there as well. Here are some of your options.

## Hire a Publicist

Believe me, even if a big publisher were to produce your book, you would still have to do marketing. I have colleagues in California whose books were produced by major publishing companies. They expected big book tours and were quite disappointed. When they did do book signings in bookstores, often very few people showed up. They ended up hiring a publicist to help them. You can do this too.

A publicist will help you put together a press kit and get you on radio, TV and into good magazines. They will get people to review your book in major newspapers, and create a buzz for your book. This can be money very well spent. These people know the territory. They can do campaigns locally, nationally and internationally. They usually charge by the hour and will try to get you a certain number of media placements. They do not guarantee book sales or speaking engagements.

## Hire a Marketing Expert

A marketing expert can help you create a marketing plan. You will need one if you want to promote your book. He or she can also help you implement the plan, for a fee. Perhaps you can negotiate a percentage arrangement. This can work very well if you are selling more expensive products such as CD sets, home study programs, workshops, seminars and speeches.

There are many people offering these kinds of services. Choose one with a track record.

## The Less Expensive Way

There are lists of radio talk shows that regularly interview authors. Both big city and small town talk radio stations all over Canada and the

United States are crying for new people to interview, particularly authors. M. Scott Peck, the author of, *The Road Less Traveled*, kept his book on bestseller lists for 12 years. How? He vowed to be on talk radio three times per week. Imagine, just 15 minutes a day, in your jammies.

Get a list, hire a publicist or an otherwise good writer to help you develop a media release, and hire your spouse, your teenager, or a summer student to smile and dial, talk to the producers, and get you on the radio. You can even make the calls yourself. If your book is not in bookstores all over North America, no matter. When you are on the radio, give them the 800 number that you acquired just for this purpose, that you, your spouse, your child, or a summer student will answer, and fill orders from your garage. A colleague made $250,000.00 this way, without spending five cents on advertising.

## Do a Massive Internet Campaign

A colleague of mine, with books and CDs to sell, made over $250,000.00 in one year through massive e-mail campaigns. All you have to do is develop a fantastic sales letter, be prepared to offer a couple of freebees, and find ways to get access to 200,000 e-mail addresses.

I am not being facetious. My colleague did it and you can too. You can attempt to develop that e-mail list yourself, which will take you quite a while, or you can partner with like-minded people, people who have done it before, pay a fee for the use of their list or, if feasible, offer them a percentage. You really need to think outside the box on this one. You need to think about who is influential in your field and have the courage to approach them about partnering. My colleague who did this is Peggy McColl and she teaches people how to do what she did. Find out all about her at www.peggymccoll.com.

## The Other Moneymaking, Change-the-World Way

Get on the speaking circuit. Yes, some people fear public speaking more than death, but if you are a published author, you need to get over your fear of being out there.

## Toastmasters, CAPS and NSA

Join Toastmasters or attend a few guest meetings of your local chapter of The Canadian Association of Professional Speakers (CAPS) or the National Speakers Association (NSA) in the United States. Toastmasters helps people learn the mechanics of public speaking, while CAPS and NSA are associations of experts in various fields who speak professionally as the major part of their income stream. CAPS and NSA will teach you more advanced platform mechanics and the business of speaking. You will also get to rub shoulders with people who have been in the business a long time and can mentor you. Being a member of CAPS or NSA is worth its weight in solid gold and is a networking and learning opportunity that you should not pass up if you are serious about selling your books and acquiring speaking engagements internationally. The more you give, the more you get. Join a committee. Get on the board. Let people see who you are, and don't be afraid to ask for what you want and need. CAPS and NSA are also part of the International Speakers Federation, partnering with sister associations in places such as Australia and Great Britain. CAPS and NSA can open up the whole world to you.

## Get a Speaking Coach

Get someone to help you, if necessary, and develop both half-hour speeches and three-hour seminars on your book. If your local CAPS or NSA chapter has an apprenticeship program, take it. Learn how to speak and how to get bookings. You can learn even faster by hiring a coach or partnering with a colleague who does this well. You don't have to go it alone. Let others who are experts help you in this area.

## Practice for Free

Your local Rotary, Lions, Optimists, Chamber of Commerce, and Breakfast Networking Meeting groups need speakers. Volunteer. You will be doing them a service and serving yourself as well. Plus, you will begin to be seen in the community as an expert who has written a book. Do not be shy to ask for the sale. I have seen too many speakers with books speak for free at these meetings and forget to tell people that they have books for sale.

## Homework:

Who are the publicists in your area, what services do they offer and how much do they charge?

_____

_____

_____

_____

If you need help developing a marketing plan, who can help you? What are their services and how much do they charge?

_____

_____

_____

_____

Develop a marketing plan, either on your own or with help.

Join Toastmasters and CAPS or NSA.

Book yourself five free speaking engagements.

| Who | Where | Date |
|-----|-------|------|
| 1. | | |
| 2. | | |
| 3. | | |
| 4. | | |
| 5. | | |

# Fare Thee Well

So, now you have taken the time to listen to the gnawing voice inside that told you to write a book. You have explored why you wanted to write, who you were writing for, and how they would be different after they read your book. You have set your book up on your computer and put in the time to write and edit your work until you feel that you have done your best. You have worked with editors, graphic artists and printers to create the most pleasing packaging possible.

You have joined Toastmasters and CAPS or NSA and explored developing a marketing plan and hiring a publicist.

Now it is time to let your light shine and, in so doing, help others to shine also. Have fun, and may you have many blessings and bring blessings to others, too, now that you have taken the time to *Write that Book.*

# Endnotes

1   Frankl, Viktor, *Man's Search for Meaning*, Washington Square Press, New York, 1894.

2   Mazlow, Abraham, *The Farther Reaches of Human Nature*, Viking, New York, 1971.

3   Williamson, Serena, *Two Voices/Circle of Love*, White Knight Publications, Toronto, 2003.

4   Rolbin, Sharon (AKA Serena Williamson), *Surviving Organizational Insanity: Keeping Spirit Alive at Work*, Lightkeeper Publishing, Ottawa, 1996.

5   Garrow, Robert F., Ahoy Mates! *Leadership Lessons from Successful Pirates*, Book Coach Press, Ottawa, 2003.

6   Duncan, Heather, *There's Always Something You Can Do: Women's Engaging Stories and Your Financial Future*, Book Coach Press, Ottawa, 2003.

7   Levine, Stephen, *A Year to Live: How to Live this Year as if it Were Your Last*, Bell Tower, New York, 1997.

8   Jennings, Susan, *Save Some for Me: Inspiration for Single Mothers and the People Who Love Them*, Book Coach Press, Ottawa, 2003.

9   Urichuck, Bob, *Online for Life: The Twelve Disciplines for Living Your Dreams*, Creative Bound, Ottawa, 2000.

10  Mager, Robert, *Goal Analysis, Goal Analysis: How to Clarify Your Goals So You Can Actually Achieve Them*, Kogan Page, New York, 1990.

11  Thomas Yaccato, Joanne, *Balancing Act: Canadian Woman's Financial Success Guide*, Prentice Hall Canada, Scarborough, 1999.

12  Nathanson, Craig, *P is for Perfect: Your Perfect Vocational Day*, Book Coach Press, Ottawa, 2003.

13  Poynter, Dan, *Writing Nonfiction: Turning Thoughts Into Books*, Para Publishing, Santa Barbara, 2000.

14  Page, Susan, *The Shortest Distance Between You and a Published Book*, Broadway Books, New York, 1997.

15  Larsen, Michael, *How to Write a Book Proposal*, 2nd Edition, Writer's Digest Books, Cincinnati, Ohio, 1997.

16  McQuinn, Allyson, *The Path to Cure*, Book Coach Press, Ottawa, 2004.

**Book Coach Press**
is dedicated to helping prospective
authors make a difference by getting the message
that is inside of them out into the world.

Books and other products
designed to get the book out of you
can be found on our website,
**www.BookCoachPress.com**

For information about our personalized
coaching, editing, speaking and
book-writing groups contact us at
**info@BookCoachPress.com**

We will be happy to design a program
that suits you best, so you too can
**WRITE THAT BOOK**